...AND YOUR POINT IS?

How to stop killing your clients with PowerPoint
poisoning and deliver presentations that
provoke and persuade

Note for Librarians: A cataloguing record for this book is available from Library and Archives Canada at www.collectionscanada.ca/amicus/index-e.html
ISBN 1-4120-9241-8

Printed in Victoria, BC, Canada. Printed on paper with minimum 30% recycled fibre.
Trafford's print shop runs on "green energy" from solar, wind and other environmentally-friendly power sources.

TRAFFORD
PUBLISHING™
Offices in Canada, USA, Ireland and UK

Book sales for North America and international:
Trafford Publishing, 6E–2333 Government St.,
Victoria, BC V8T 4P4 CANADA
phone 250 383 6864 (toll-free 1 888 232 4444)
fax 250 383 6804; email to orders@trafford.com
Book sales in Europe:
Trafford Publishing (UK) Limited, 9 Park End Street, 2nd Floor
Oxford, UK OX1 1HH UNITED KINGDOM
phone 44 (0)1865 722 113 (local rate 0845 230 9601)
facsimile 44 (0)1865 722 868; info.uk@trafford.com
Order online at:
trafford.com/06-0995

10 9 8 7 6 5 4

*To my mother, whose constant correction of
my speech and grammar as a child led to unexpected
results in the adult*

Table of Contents

Special Acknowledgement

It would be disingenuous of us not to acknowledge from the outset the outstanding service that Dr. Edward Tufte, Professor Emeritus of Yale, has done in awakening us all to the truly disastrous consequences that can ensue when PowerPoint is improperly used.

Dr. Tufte, whom many regard as our country's foremost expert on visualizing information, is chiefly responsible for discovering and then publicizing the culture of non-communication at a huge government agency that resulted in a national tragedy. And we all must give Dr. Tufte his due when he concludes that a PowerPoint presentation was indeed at the heart of a series of unrecognized problems that might have been more readily discovered had other forms of inter-departmental knowledge transfer been used. We also must state that seeing Dr. Tufte, the author of seven plus books, perform in person, with his talent to break virtually all the rules of proper presentation skills and still keep his audience with him at every step, inspired us to stay the course with producing this book.

We believe that throughout this book we have properly credited Dr. Tufte with all of his insights with which we agree and have thus passed on to readers. (For those we may have missed, we'll defer to the professor's advice to information designers, "Don't be original, be right!")

Foreword

One cold winter morning not too long ago, a group of highly educated specialists working for a large American corporation came to a terrifying conclusion: events from the previous week had created a much more dangerous situation than anyone realized, and it was up to them to alert decision makers from above of the lingering doom.

The decision makers, also very highly educated people, at first rebuffed the experts, claiming there simply wasn't enough evidence for concern. But the experts pressed on, and ultimately the higher-ups challenged them to formally present their findings.

In the presentation that ensued, the experts included all the data and information necessary to make their point – or so they thought. The problem was, although their presentation contained everything anyone needed to know to realize the problem was, indeed, as dire as the experts predicted, the information was not presented in a format that facilitated an unambiguous realization of the truth.

As a result, the decision makers did not take the recommendations of the experts; no action was taken, and no one even deemed it necessary to inform the potential victims that something might be awry. Shortly there-after, seven people died.

This is a truly tragic story, made all the more so by the fact that for this particular organization, it was the second time that decision makers failed to heed the warnings of their own experts. And yet as you will see, the failure in communication resulted not so much from the *content* of the information presented, but rather the *form* in which it was presented.

As is so often the case, the people who put together this presentation knew their material cold, and assumed that as long as they laid out all the facts, their audience couldn't help but come to the conclusions that they themselves had. But content is not only just one part of a successful presentations, it happens to be the smallest component of what creates impact in the mind of the audience. In order to make a point from the platform, the presenter also needs to *appear* confident and comfortable with the content. And in order for that to happen, certain indispensable design parameters must be met.

At the end of this book, we'll take a look at an actual slide from the presentation that doomed these seven souls, and if you indeed read and take to heart the rules we uncover here, you will be able to see for yourself the reasons the experts failed to make their case.

You see, the experts' presentation did not convince the critical decision makers in the audience for a simple, but all too common reason: the presentation designers failed to follow seven simple rules that guarantee audiences will follow your arguments and get your point. But your next presentation doesn't have to fail, because in this book, you will learn the seven rules of successful slide design.

That's right – in just eleven chapters you will learn to save your presentations from the fate of 99% of all business presentations today – audience overload. Audience overload occurs when visuals contain not just too much information, but too much of the kind of information the brain does not readily absorb.

And yet, of the literally thousands of slides we at PublicSpeakingSkills.com see every year, 99% of all slides contain more information than the average (and even above-average) person can discern before the presenters moves on to, "Next slide, please!"

"If you had to identify, in one word, the reason why the human race has not achieved, and never will achieve, its full potential, that word would be: 'meetings'."

— Dave Barry

Chapter 1

Introduction

Why we are here and
what we will learn

This book was written in response to participants of our firm's *Advanced Presentation Design* course who asked to have all that they've learned codified into a format they could pass along to friends and colleagues. (For their encouragement to complete this project, we are grateful.)

In the course of this book, you will dramatically increase your ability to communicate ideas by (1) taking presentation design theory to the next level, and (2) studying examples of the latest technologies. At the same time, you will learn new techniques to produce great works of classic design, rather than using technology for *technology's sake..*

Upon completing this book you will know how to:
- Discern the essences of Good Design and how it benefits your life
- Understand how the brain processes Visual Input
- Properly Deliver Visual Information
- Make information flow - how Less is More, and Timing is Everything
- Use eye contact, gestures, and body language for maximum effect
- Develop and organize a presentation for any audience and any event
- Design visuals to enhance both your message & performance
- Design graphs that clearly & honestly display the relationship of data
- Deliver visuals in a way that the audience is in sync and on the point

Getting through the roadblocks

If you've never taken a course in presentation design, then you can't be blamed for not knowing that there's a very simple, surefire way of getting around the filtering process most audiences use to screen new information.

When you learn to by-pass the filters, your audiences absorb your arguments instantly – and unambiguously. This was where the experts failed in the tragic story of the misunderstood presentation – a story that you'll hear in full at the end of this book.

These filters are just one of the roadblocks to true knowledge transfer that presenters throw up with the approach most take to visual design. But wait – it gets worse!

Mimicking Your Boss's Mistakes

Because most business presenters are given a laptop and a copy of PowerPoint and told to give a presentation *tomorrow*, most presentations are made by mimicking the boss's mistakes – after all, if it's good enough for the boss, it's good enough for me, right? So the template most presenters use is based on one created by somebody who very likely never took a course or read a book on presentation design, but rather was simply also mimicking what she had seen when she was trying to impress *her* boss. And with each progression up the corporate ladder, the situation repeats – and the problems compound.

Our firm has been working with people from all different industries for over a decade to help them improve, among other things, their presentation delivery skills. And every year, our job has become more difficult, because presenters come to us from corporate cultures that have developed evermore complicated – read "incomprehensible" – corporate presentations that not only make their jobs more difficult, but also cruelly bear the approval of upper management.

The main point of this book is to clearly establish the relationship between proper design and proper delivery techniques. The sad truth is that while many people are sent to training classes to learn presentation delivery skills, all the skills in the world won't help them if they're trying to deliver the "wrong" presentation.

In order to be effective, a presenter must understand a number of rules about proper presentation delivery. Foremost of these are the basic laws of eye-contact. *But proper eye-contact can only occur if the presentation is designed to allow it.* In chapter 8, you will learn to design slides that not only foster proper eye-contact, but also assure that the *audience and presenter are on the same wave-length every step of the way.*

It's About Them

You'll also discover exactly what happens every time the presenter clicks to a new slide. Most presenters assume that the audience willingly awaits their escort through the intricacies of the slide, when in fact, that's the last thing they do!

There is only one thing that ever interests any audience member, and if it's not in your slide, you're not going to get your point across, no matter how important, essential, or life-threatening you might believe it to be.

As computer-based presentations have become the norm, audiences are being overwhelmed with productions that seem to use every feature and font that the presenter can find. You may think your presentation skills are great and the audience is with you as they politely nod their heads and smile, but beware: the emperor believed that only a "fool" couldn't see his beautiful new clothes!

Figure 1.1 We should have known we were in trouble back then. Back cover pitch tells us this new product allows us to "create multi-level bullet charts, word charts, annotated diagrams, tables, or any combination with ease and effectiveness".

Few corporate audience members are willing to stand up and declare that they really can't see anything they understand in your presentation. But if you couldn't follow the last slide show you sat through, much less stay awake, ask yourself if your own presentation designs might use a little help, too.

Read this book, and you will learn a "paint-by-numbers" approach to proper presentation design; in the process, you will save your next audience from the insidious new corporate syndrome, "Death by PowerPoint".

A Short History

In 1984, former Berkeley PhD. student Bob Gaskins left his job as head of computer research at Bell-Northern Research and joined another Mountain View, California software firm, Forethought, Incorporated in return for limited monetary

Figure 1.2 The product-improvements in this edition included the ability to import "spreadsheet data from Lotus 1-2-3...Microsoft Excel...or comma or tab-deliminated ASCII files". The beginning of the 8-point font slide.

compensation and a good deal of company stock. In hindsight, Forethought was a good move. That same year,

Fig 1.3 *"For everyone who can't wait to get a good idea across".* Were they suggesting that instead of taking the time to create good content, we should just use screeching brakes?

in cooperation with software developer Dennis Austin, they began work on a program they originally called Presenter. Years later, Gaskins would find an old business plan from that time describing the concept behind the new software. One phrase read, *"Allows the content-originator to control the presentation."*

PowerPoint 1.0 was launched in April 1987, a Macintosh-only product that allowed non-programmers to put together simple black-and-white overheads without the need for a corporate graphics department. Later that same year Gaskins and his colleagues sold Forethought to Microsoft for cash and stock.

Modern business would never be the same. Immediately, business presenters who had little or no background in design fundamentals were now able to do what thousands of recently empowered "desktop" publishers could do: produce very technically competent garbage.

The software improved over time, and new products made by competing companies offered increasingly sophisticated and sometimes useful enhancements.

Eventually, it became apparent to some that instead of simply designing ever more impressive overheads, what this new genre was really about was its ability to be a means to itself - that the computer was no longer the design *machine*, the computer was the presentation! Now with each new version of computer-based presentation software we find

Figure 1.4
"Illustrrate your ideas with dramatic Microsoft OfficeArt text and drawing tools, including flowchart symbols, Bezier curves, and 3-D effects".

new ways to dazzle and impress ourselves with words and pictures in the dynamic environment of an LCD screen or projected image.

Unfortunately, good software alone does not make a good presentation. In fact, quite the opposite! You will learn that there are strict rules to follow, and many pitfalls that can sap the strength of even superb speakers, ruining an otherwise decent show. Although speaking in public comes easily to some but is difficult for most, *many who struggle with public speaking are simply trying to deliver the "wrong" presentation.*

Throughout this book you will be treated to examples of the typical slides we see followed by examples of ways to improve them. If you see a lot of your own work in the "before" slides, don't be disheartened. Although many presenters have taken a course in how to use PowerPoint or other presentation software, very few have had the opportunity to actually take a course in presentation *design.* As we will see, good design makes all the difference.

No Experience Necessary

And, it does not take any special talent you have to be born with. There are rules to follow, all quite simple, and all quite easy to learn. In fact, you will see that a properly designed presentation takes less time to develop, not more. A good presentation rarely needs more than four or five "mini-templates" from which you create all the other slides in your presentation. Continuity is the order of the day, and so most of your slides should have the same look, and transition in the same way, with only the content changing from one slide to the next.

You will learn a "paint-by-numbers" approach to good design, and how to save your next audience from the new corporate syndrome, *"Death by PowerPoint"*.

As it is our course, book content is divided into modules that thoroughly cover professional presentation theory; designing slides to be delivered; content that works; delivery with visuals; the mechanics of advanced presentation design; handling charts and graphs; and finally, innovating.

Not just 'How' but also 'Why?'

With a firm understanding of *why* the design principles work, you will then be taken to the practical application module - the "How to do it" part. However, this book is not a primer in PowerPoint! Instead, we look to advance the art of presentation design by clearly demonstrating why some features of the software work to enhance the impact and clarity of your message, and why most (almost all) do not.

Even if you have only a limited practical knowledge of the software, you will nevertheless learn what *can* be done, and you'll jumpstart your understanding of its potential. In fact, if you have never designed a computer-based presentation and are now reading this book, you are an extremely fortunate individual! Like a newbie golfer, you won't have to waste any time unlearning bad habits.

Best of all, you will discover that you need not be a graphic artist to create understandable and persuasive on-screen results.

We always relish the opportunity to train presentation design to people who have little or no experience with PowerPoint. One such group we trained recently was embarrassed (they told us later) to admit they had never created an on-screen presentation before. They had been loosing many contracts because they had to present to clients with flipcharts and photographs against the competition's multi-media shows.

During a 2-hour workshop phase, we were amazed to see that all of their presentations conformed to the rules, and actually looked quite professional. Shortly after the class, they began winning contracts even with higher bids. Their clients told them the polish and clarity of their presentations really set them apart from the competition, and were a major factor in winning the contract. They were delighted at this, of course, and sent us copies of their winning presentations. We admit we felt quite proud of our "honor students".

The key here was that having never created an on-screen presentation prior to the class, they never knew what to do *wrong*, and they had never been influenced by the bad designs of colleagues.

A Cultural Thing

We have found over the years, it is common for presentations throughout the corporation to look and feel the same, with all the same elements of bad design and content. Many at the corporate level continue to create according to what they've seen before, never even considering that the original "template" was no doubt put together by someone with no training! Sometimes it's true that what you don't know CAN hurt you.

TMI

Finally, you must understand this: in order to get your audience to buy in to your message, you must prepare and deliver it in a way consistent with adult learning theory. That means you must understand the limits to how much information an audience member can absorb at one time, and what form that information must take in order to first attract, and then keep, their attention.

Of the literally thousands of slides our firm receives for review and revision each year, almost all share the same basic problem: *Too Much Information!* TMI leads directly to *too little retention.* Too much, too soon, keys the audience's brain to brace for overload. That gets their natural defense mechanisms jumping into action. Rather than allow you to control their information uptake, overloaded audiences begin to pick and choose what information they will absorb, based on the parts of your message they view as meaningful to them. You, of course, never know what they have rejected or ignored.

The rules of proper presentation design that we preach in this book all exist to ensure that neither you nor your audience suffers from the effects of trying to deal with TMI at one time. When that happens,

Educating Your Audience

Fred Pryor, often billed as 'the father of the one-day seminar', and a considered expert on adult learning, was fond of saying, "Training is selling, and selling is training".

Figure 1.5 TMI: Most of our clients cringe when they see this slide, because it so reminds them of their own!

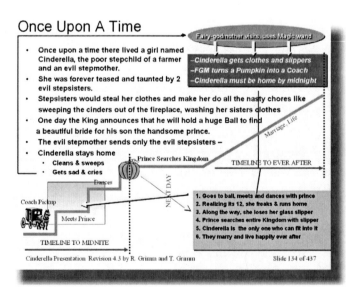

That is, if you're doing it right, you never lose sight of the fact that while training adults, you must be constantly checking your audience for buy-in. In the same way, to sell effectively, you want others to reach conclusions 'on their own'; the best way to do this is to lead them to the conclusion you want by 'educating' them as to what course provides their best solution.

PowerPoint is a really marvelous tool for creating this training/selling environment, because when used properly, the presenter can lead the audience down the desired path one step at a time. Just as a good trial attorney "builds" his case by laying out the facts one on top of the other, a good presenter can use the tools of proper presentation design to win the case every time.

> *"All truth goes through three steps:*
> *First, it is ridiculed.*
> *Second, it is violently opposed.*
> *Finally, it is accepted as self-evident".*
> - Arthur Schopenhauer

Summary

- Audiences are always skeptical of new information
- Corporate cultures keep bad habits alive
- Talent is not required – respect for design is
- Most slides overwhelm both audience & presenter

Chapter 2

The Value of Good Design

Good presentations begin with
awareness of good (and bad) design

The Good, The Bad, and The Mediocre

Bill Stumpf, social curmudgeon and designer of the Aeron chair, is quite succinct in his definition of design:

"If I'm going to talk about design, that purely arbitrary and immensely human construct, I should say that by design I mean the process both physical and mental by which people give order to objects, community, environments, and behavior. Like many hard-to-define but profoundly important activities, design is both art and science. It aims to make our existence more meaningful, connect us to natural realities, show us the advantages of graceful restraint, infuse serious work with playful humor, extend human capacity—physical and emotional and spiritual. Designers make ideas into things."

Your job as a presentation designer is to make ideas into visual images.

To gain an appreciation of how good design adds to the quality of our lives, it helps to look at some examples of truly bad design that we all deal with on an everyday basis. Bad design abounds, and everyday our lives are a little less pleasant for it.

The really unfortunate thing about poorly designed objects is that countless unpleasant times might have been spared if only the designer had thought through his or her approach a little more thoroughly.

A Fine Line

The line between good and bad design is often fine. It can be no more than placement of a button in a spot not easily accessed by mistake; a label placed where it could actually be seen before the wrong action is taken; a multi-step process where you don't have to get to step seven before you realize you did step three wrong; or a lever or handle shaped more like the movement it wants you to make.

When you acquire a more developed sensitivity to design, you begin to look at all things with questions such as, "Might it have been better to do it *this* way?", or "What would it have taken to make it work like *this?*"

Then take a look at the last presentation you delivered. Do you suppose there were elements that caused even temporary confusion? And then when you explained the element, did they say, "Oh I get it - but why didn't you just say it *this* way?"?

Back to Buttocks

All bad designs cause the expenditure of more effort to produce the same result. The more effort it takes to *absorb* your message, the less energy is available for *processing* the message itself. Effort causes discomfort. In the presentation environment, that can mean disaster because -for the very same reason- discomfort leads to disassociation from the message. That's why professional trainers make certain the learning environment is as comfortable as possible - fresh water, good seats, frequent breaks. "The mind can only absorb what the buttocks can endure" is old but still relevant. Bad presentation design is a pain in the ass, and it stops message uptake just as quickly.

Everyday things

Now let's step back from presentations for a few moments.

Think about the various devices - electrical, mechanical, architectural, digital, whatever – that you use or come in contact with on a daily or weekly basis. Keep in mind that anything manufactured for human consumption was first designed by a human. You know that some humans are more talented than others. If you're like most people, you have probably been annoyed or frustrated with a device than was designed by one from the less talented group.

Unfortunately, the more you learn about design, the more you begin to realize that bad design permeates our lives. The only good news is that the problem with things not working the way they should is not you – it's the design.

Ain't technology grand?

In our *Advanced Presentation Design* class, we start off the day by soliciting from participants the one device that drives them crazy, and ask them to explain why. You can probably relate to most of them. Five years ago, computers and VCR's led the list; today it is cell phones. Cell phones are especially insidious, because they lead you to believe that the technology actually works, and then when you come to depend on that technology, it invariably lets you down.

In the year 2005, somewhere around 60 million Americans owned cell phones, and a little over 2 dozen knew how to use their every feature. Have you ever had a bad experience with your cell phone? How long did it take you to learn its system? And when you finally felt you had reasonable command of its technology, did you break it or lose it and have to buy a new one with a completely different system?

Remember When?

Good old Western Electric telephones and Underwood typewriters had keys and buttons that, when activated, achieved a singular result. Cell phones and computers have *operating systems* behind their buttons and keys. Before you can get them to produce your desired result, you have to learn and comprehend their underlying operating systems. Few functions are self-evident.

Automated Teller Machines are another good example of devices we are forced to deal with that fail at both the design and the operating level. Conceived and designed by that great humanitarian group, bankers, as a selfless expression of their desire to provide with us ultimate convenience, ATM's are tolerated only because at the end of the process they give us what we all really want and need, now. Only bankers could create a machine for de-humanizing a system (customers getting money from a teller) and in the process dehumanize the customer as well.

Start with design: Ever found a drive-up ATM where the keys on the machine matched the functions on the screen?

Figure 2.1 If you've ever been frustrated even just trying to find the right keys on your local ATM, you're not alone.

In most cases, the Yes or NO arrows point perfectly between two keys. "Enter your four-digit identification number and then press this key" - Which key? This key or that key? Why do some functions require you touch the screen, and others that you press keys? Then when you take your money, and you're putting it in your wallet, it asks if you want another transaction, but if you say no, it immediately starts beeping to get you to remove your card. Wouldn't a second or two to get your hand from one part of the machine to the other be nice before being blasted by a beeper?

Jumping through hoops

Perhaps the greatest insult from these modern-day necessities is the disrespect they have for your time. Having saved themselves from the hourly rates they used to pay tellers, banks felt it was important, from a design standpoint, to devalue your time altogether. So in order for you to get your money now, you get to jump through hoops.

After asking for your PIN, you are presented with a menu of six to eight functions from which to choose. Ninety-five per cent of all ATM transactions are to get cash; why isn't that a first-page default, with only the other functions requiring additional keystrokes?

Next you have to tell the machine what account you want it from; again ninety-five percent of all transactions involve the primary checking account. Is your ATM card tied to your *secondary* and *tertiary* accounts as well? Finally, we are insulted with the suggestion that having done all this, we can halt the whole process now if we don't want to pay a fee. And of course it's not until we press the "I accept your &%$* fee" button we're informed that the cardholder's PIN does not match their records, please try again.

Bad design not only requires more effort, it requires more time - your time. Most people's time is precious, so they appreciate it when others show respect for their time, and are annoyed when they don't.

Figure 2.2 Why can't ATM screens look like this?

More mundane atrocities

Our class participants find annoyances and delays in even mundane everyday devices.

We hear about cords on vacuum cleaners - as long as they've been around, designers have still been able to specify them to be only one of two sizes - too short or too long. Either length, they're always in the way. And what's with the "new" concepts for the on-off switch they come up with for each new model? Why are they always so counter-intuitive that both their location and operation have to be rediscovered with every use?

Quality of life issues abound in the simplest of devices. How about in public buildings with double sets of doors that open in one direction for the first set, the opposite for the next, and whose handle shapes don't visually suggest the way they work? New CD packages require that you break something before you can play the one song on the disc that you paid for the whole CD just to hear! So on top of that insult, you now either slice through the jewel-case with a knife or split off the tip of your fingernail. And by the time you get through all the "anti-theft" wrappings on DVD packages, it's usually too late to watch the movie.

How often do you find a stove that you haven't used before that unambiguously identifies which knob works which burner? In a hotel room, do you always know which way to turn the single shower lever to get hot? And even if you can figure it out well enough to get into the shower, can you instantly find cold when your roommate flushes the toilet? Many spigot designers incorporate labels to identify or describe their function; but generally speaking, if a design requires a label, it wasn't designed right in the first place.

Can you get water into and coffee out of your drip-style coffee-maker without spilling any of either? Where does your refrigerator spew more ice – into your glass or onto the floor? Can your friends operate your microwave without your showing them how?

Figure 2.3 Next time you use your hair-dryer, notice whether the high-low switch works the way you would expect, or to affect a High setting you need to push the switch to its Lower position.

The list of design-challenged items that we endure is endless, and although it would be fun to go on and discuss them all, that is not the entire scope of this book. Rather, discussing how design affects our everyday lives is purposeful in getting you to think very hard about how your designs affect the people you subject them too, and why it *is* worth the effort. And although it is kind and thoughtful to design in ways that enhance, rather than detract from the quality of your audience's experience, the bottom line is simple: good design goes down easier.

You need every opportunity to get your audience on your side, and you must allow nothing in your control to discomfort the people you're trying to persuade. As Edward Tufte says, "audiences are fragile; respect them".

Whose fault is it, anyway?

One last sad truth about bad design is that so many people who are frustrated by it think it's *their* fault! When people don't understand what they're told, or audiences don't understand what they see on the screen, they often blame themselves – they believe that they're either stupid or slow or perhaps they simply learn in other ways.

Coming from a technical training background, it has long been apparent to us that people who have difficulty getting computers to do what they want tend to take the difficulty upon themselves. When a file won't save or a network won't connect or an indecipherable warning messages pops up, there's a natural human tendency to believe that it's *my* fault, that *I* did something wrong, that *I* don't understand what is obviously easily understood by everybody else.

Did you know that software engineers not only know this, but also actually *count* on it when deciding how much time and effort to devote to the debugging process? Many software companies can't afford to beta test new applications with thousands of users, and so they never discover just how many things can go wrong with it until it has been on the market for some time. So rather than create an error messages that says:

they are content to let you think that somehow, somewhere,

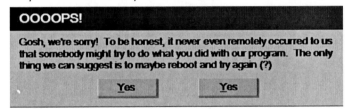

Figure 2.4 Believe it or not, most of the time your computer doesn't do what yu want it to, *it's not your fault!*

you did something that you shouldn't have done, and that you don't understand computers enough to argue with someone who knows enough to actually design programs!

Cliff's Philosophy...

The reason it usually takes a study of bad design to understand good design is simple: Good design often produces as its main end product a "lack of awareness". That is, when something is designed properly, it will often execute its function in a way that doesn't grab our attention – it simply works.

Throughout the 1980's, the situation comedy *Cheers* was one of the most widely watched television shows of all time in the U.S. When it finally came to the end of its run, the network and the media touted the closing episode for months. When the final day came, the hype around the show was that it would really go out with a bang – a show no couch potato could afford to miss.

In the end, the show was less than memorable – except for the closing line. Cliff, the philosopher mail carrier, let us all in on the secret to happiness in life. It all came down to "comfortable shoes" – anyone can be happy as long as they wear comfortable shoes. Of course, a mail carrier might have a strong opinion on that!

Why ask why?

Not everybody found that message a satisfying sendoff for the most popular show ever, but it spoke deeply to people who take design seriously: to be really comfortable, shoes must be designed to not cause you any pain. In other words, bad shoes hurt your feet and cause painful awareness – with every step. Well-designed shoes never speak to you. They do their job quietly so you can do yours.

So when we get in a car and put our morning coffee into a cup holder that comes easily to hand and keeps our laps dry and our knuckles unskinned, we rarely think about how much time and effort might have gone into getting the holders' action and location just right. It's only when we find a cup holder that blocks our access to the radio or that's not really deep enough to securely hold our Supersized drink do we ask ourselves, "Why on earth did they design it *this* way?"

It's a shame, really, that our reaction to design is much like our reaction to kids - the bad ones get attention while those who behave we tend to ignore and allow to play by themselves. We often curse the device that doesn't work, but rarely do we find ourselves speaking fondly to common objects that do things very well. That doesn't mean we shouldn't be looking for good design in common places. Constant awareness is essential to discovering the subtleties of design. In order to be good designers, we need to know what it is about a properly designed object that makes it work, even when it's not announcing itself.

Working together

Next time you walk around the space where you live, take note of how well the different components work together. Begin with the doors. Do doors always open the way you would expect? Do doors in proximity to each other keep out of each other's way? Do closets open to allow the easiest possible access from where you usually approach them, or do you have to walk around the door first? Does the placement of doors afford the path of least resistance through your space, or do you often expend excess energy to get to where you want to go?

What about your systems? Do light switches fall to hand in a dark room, or must you always stumble in darkness before reaching them? Are they all in the same relative position in each room, or must you learn their position every time? How about the placement of the switches themselves within the switchbox - can you intuit which light a particular switch will activate based on its position? What about your thermostat - is it easy to maintain your desired environment or are you constantly going out of your way to access it? Are plumbing functions discretely obscured, or are living room guests privy to all activity? Are phone jacks placed in areas most likely to facilitate making a phone call, or do you have to use very long cords?

Lost in Space

Finally, how well does your dwelling embrace the universe? That is, does it make the most of possible orientations to the compass, so that adverse effects of summer heat and winter cold are minimized? Are windows placed where they will enhance lighting and/or views, or do you often wish one were moved this way or that? Can your driveway get help from the sun to melt the snow, or does its angle to the sun keep ice there well into spring? Can natural breezes cool the interior without the help of noisy fans?

Not all places where we live were designed for the betterment of the life of the inhabitants, of course. Cost often gets in the way. Unfortunately, its more often a lack of skill than lack of funds that results in spaces that make us "work" to use them. Residential architectural design is all about knowing not just what we need, but *how we use it*, everyday. It's about the interaction, and like everything else in good design, the less effort required to achieve the desired function, the better our quality of life.

Better presentations

Ask yourself: Do your presentations have a less-than-evident operating system? Before someone can get your message (the function of your presentation) do they first have to learn and comprehend your design?

Your main goal when designing a presentation should be to keep your audience's attention on your idea, your pitch, your proposal---your message. They should never be distracted by, or even really aware of, your design. Dazzling them with bells and whistles will help them remember the bells and whistles, *not* your message. You need to make your message the star so that nothing takes their minds away from it.

Single slides with Too Much Information splattered on them require much more time for both you and the audience to process than if the same information were thoughtfully spread out over several slides. Do you suppose there is a relationship between how an audience feels (annoyed or appreciative) and how accepting they are of your message?

If you spend time looking at things from a design standpoint, you will begin to think in terms of how good the product is by how well it does its job without bragging about it. You'll be asking yourself whether this element or that element is really essential to the task, or whether it's just "decoration". In good design, decoration distracts. Your slides need to provide information in a compelling way, but without decoration.

Increase your awareness to design, and you will create better presentations than most people in business today.

Summary

- Fine line between good and bad design.
- Bad design requires more effort
- Too much functionality interferes with basic use
- Good design does not shout
- Don't be intimidated – It's not your fault!
- Don't decorate - Make your message the star

Chapter 3

First to Know:
What Audiences Want

Working with human nature to guarantee sync

This is where proper presentation design begins: with a fundamental understanding of what happens each time the presenter presses a button and brings up a new slide. For the vast majority of presentations we see, slide design (content and structure) does not reflect the fact that the information on the slide needs to be delivered to the audience through the presenter. And only very rarely does design begin with the perspective of the listener, in whose mind the real presentation takes place.

To understand what happens when you click to the next slide, we have to understand a very basic tenet of human nature - that is, we have a pervasive and inherent need to be "the first to know".

A 24/7 World

In the fall of 2000, when the result of the presidential election was in doubt for two months, both the CNN and USA Today websites were hawking their opt-in mailing lists that would email to recipients the final decision as soon as it was known. "Be the First to Know," shouted both come-ons for signing up.

There was a time in pre-narrowcast American culture when we were slaves to the timetables of the news providers. National news came on at 6:00 PM and ran for fifteen minutes, followed by another fifteen of local news, sports and weather. At the time, people still preferred to get their news on paper, and most large cities had morning and afternoon offerings, some cities with several.

When the technology of communications was slower, we took a more historical approach to news - news was about what happened. We were accustomed to waiting for the news, and news had a time: *Did you see the morning paper? Did you hear the evening news?*

But with electronic advancements, we came to think of news more in terms of *what is happening*. Film brought us motion, but video feeds brought us *there*. Screens eclipsed paper as the preferred venue for getting the latest. Newspapers folded, first afternoon editions and then even icons of Americana - think *Herald Tribune*. Instead of being the first source of news in the world, newspapers to survive became more feature oriented – providing interest for only less perishable and less immediate content.

Cable News Network took a huge gamble that people all over the world would watch news twenty-four hours a day - news on the people's timetable, not the providers. News on demand. Fulfillment for those with the desire to be "the first to know."

Next slide, please

What does all this have to do with presentation design? You don't need to be a news junkie to share a basic trait of humans and other intelligent animals – curiosity. Curiosity is basic to survival, and we have evolved as creatures who need to learn what we can quickly. So this same desire that humans have to be *the first to know* translates to every event that involves new information uptake. During a presentation, audience members want the same control, and are basically unwilling to wait for you, the presenter, to *help* them be the first to know.

Once the curiosity about a slide has been satisfied, audience members usually will give the presenter their attention.

Figure 3.1 When the presenter has *cleared* the slide, meaning eliminated all the curiosity about it, the audience will give him their attention.

But when a new slide first appears on the screen, all eyes, like moths to the flame, tune to the new image, and immediately begin the race to be the first to know what the slide is all about. Its not their fault! They're human!

Figure 3.2 But when new information appears, until the audiences has determined for themselves what all the elements mean, the presenter is essentially "vaporized".

And at this point you realistically might as well not be there. Oh, sure, you can act as most do and begin to describe the elements in the slide, but for all intents and purposes, it matters little what you do. You could drop your pants. You could leave the room. You could tell off-color jokes. But until the audience has determined for themselves exactly what all the data and word tracks on the screen mean to them, you have approximately 0% of their attention.

Only when every member of the audience is thoroughly convinced that they know exactly what the slide means will they lend their attention back to what you are saying.

With most of the slides you see in business presentations today, this is where the disaster begins. You see, a typical slide that we see at our firm contains so much information that a typical audience member would need more than 30 seconds just to read the material, much less absorb it. The reading process is delayed, though, because first the viewer tries to decide for herself where to begin, and which piece of information is most important. Clues to the relative value of the information are often erroneous, however, as audiences base them on properties such as the size of the type or placement on the screen.

The Same Wavelength

For this reason, you must ask yourself how long it will take the average person to discover for themselves all the information you have in your slide. The more time it takes the average person to absorb and assimilate the information they see, the greater the chance you have to lose your audience.

Summary

- Audiences need to be first-to-know
- Don't be The Vanishing Presenter
- Knowledge Transfer requires all on the same page

Chapter 4

A matter of time

Designing to the limits of
human comprehension

Because people process information at different rates, faster processors will take a shorter time and the slower processors will take longer. Before you know it, you've got an audience working at three to five different wavelengths at the same time.

Then to make things worse, most presenters start talking, explaining the slide, and thus add one more thought-path, one more wavelength, to the whole process.

The Bell Curve

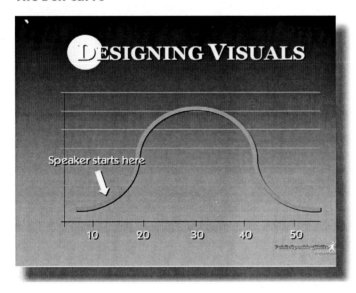

Figure 4.1 Most human group behavior can be described by a bell curve, including the amount of time it takes audience members to read and digest a slide.

Think about it. If the amount of time it takes the average reader to ingest the info on the screen is 30 seconds, then a classic bell curve will tell you that 20% of the audience is going to read it all in 20 seconds, and 20% will take 40 seconds. Another aggregate 20 will fall into the 10 to 60 second range, and before we calculate it all, we know that we have the group broken down into at least five groups of perception time-lines. Now, let's screw it all up and throw you into the soup, who then begins talking at some new, arbitrary point. To whom are you speaking?

Chance tells us you're speaking to the largest group; let's say the 40% who read at an average pace. That leaves 60% (a landslide in political terms) either way ahead or way behind the bullet point upon which he begins to expound.

But Wait! There's More!

Actually, it gets worse! You see, as much as a you might be totally in love with the design of a slide you may have spent hours composing, audiences rarely find your stuff as captivating. Because the presentation is important to you, it's easy to believe that everyone will be engrossed in the action on the screen and thus giving the event their entire attention.

But tell us: have you ever sat through a colleague's presentation and found yourself thinking about something other than the material he was sweating blood to deliver? Perhaps your plans for the upcoming weekend? The safety of your children? Whether you can let that bill slide this month?

No audience member, no matter how captivating you might believe you are, ever, ever, ever gives a presenter 100% of her attention. Human minds don't work that way. Long before Windows, we were multi-taskers.

Figure 4.2 When was the last time you tried to accomplish only one task at a time?

As lives become more complicated, and work cuts into personal time, the line between work and personal become blurred, and we compartmentalize less. Although it's difficult to attach hard numbers here, it's reasonable to assume that at best our audiences are tuning in to us -and us alone- more than 75% of the time.

So even if we're directly communicating with 40% of the group, given our (at best) 75% maximum attention factor, we have no more than 30% of the audience in our camp. The rest are either struggling to catch up, or consider themselves so advanced that their minds begin to wander to unrelated topics, such as their children, the weekend, their bills; they become non-participants in the process.

Taking it to the Limit

So what does this tell us? Of course, there is only one truly viable solution, and that is to limit, by all means possible, the amount of information that is released with each click of your mouse.

First of all, the less time it takes the audience to discern the new information, the sooner they'll get back to you and start to listen to what you really mean to "say" on the slide.

Secondly, the less time it takes the average people to figure out for themselves what's going on, the less the width of the bell curve. In other words, the less discrepancy between the fast learners and the slow.

The Proper Focus

Third, and most important, is this: if your content consists of nothing but graphics and talking points, or headline-style phrases, the audience will soon realize that they are not being shown enough information to figure things out for themselves. They will conclude that the only way they can hope to be *the first to know* is to turn their attention to you, and have it spoon fed to them. And this is exactly where you want them to be!

If you put everything you want them to know up on the screen, and if you spell it out longhand, you are training them to look to the screen for their information. Humans recognize patterns quickly, and as soon as the screen becomes the pattern, that's where they'll go. Problem is, they'll be reading one thing while you're speaking about something else!

The Bottom Line

The rule of thumb from all this? Make sure that with each passing image, it never takes longer than 10 seconds for the audience to "clear the slide". By clearing the slide we mean removing the curiosity. Have no more than 10 seconds of material - bullet point, graphic, chart, etc. - appear at one time.

Special Class

If you think your audience is more astute than average - if you think that they are somehow "special" in their ability to absorb complex concepts quickly, try testing a slide created by one specialist on another person in the same organization with a slightly different specialty.

We'll always remember training a group of pocket-protector types, one of whom protested to us that we didn't understand that they were all subject-matter experts and thus could comprehend slides with huge volumes of information. At which point one of his colleagues burst out, *"John, you've been showing that slide for three months now, and I gotta tell you, I don't have a clue what the hell it means!"*

Just because you know your subject matter intimately, don't think anybody else does. You see, regardless of their level of technical expertise, all audience members are still subject to the 75% rule. And, they all listen to same station, WII-FM – What's In It For Me? Thus, they are inherently limited by the amount of understanding and interpretation they will have of any slide not composed and conducted by themselves.

Death by PowerPoint

We actually love doing the corporate training thing with engineer types more than anyone, because these are the groups who always reach the strongest, the most endearing epiphanies about their presentation designs when they finally *do* get it.

Some years ago, we were engaged to do multiple days of training with a huge software engineering firm, the largest company by far in their field of manufacturing-design process software solutions. We actually closed the deal by convincing them that we had superior expertise in the presentation *design* aspect of presentation skills training.

Our contact, the guy in charge of choosing between the many presentation skills vendors they had contacted, was the first person from whom we heard the term, "*Death by PowerPoint*". [This was years before the now famous Dilbert slide]. He knew that their engineers were literally killing their customers with slide design that quickly, mercilessly produced brain buffer overflow.

Gone in 60 Seconds

As with the design itself, if you want the audience to remain in sync at all times, you must be able to *deliver* the material as it appears on the screen in 10 seconds or less, and for western cultures, working top-to-bottom, left-to-right.

This 10-second rule is not just a good idea. Rather, it is really the foundation upon which all the other rules are based. If your design conforms to this rule, it must conform to all the others, because violating the other rules of content and design will invariably cause you to take more than 10 seconds to "clear" the slide, or, if you are using builds, to clear the individual component.

Unfortunately, it is rare to see slides from corporate America that come anywhere near this rule. As an important part of the service that PublicSpeakingSkills.com provides its corporate clients, we review literally thousands of PowerPoint slides every year. Barely one in a hundred comes close to being able to be covered in the requisite time; instead, it usually takes 30 to 60 seconds or more for the audience to decipher the material! And in 60 seconds, they're gone!

The sad fact here is that if you accept that under the best of circumstances you have but 75% of the audiences' attention, you cannot afford to lose them even once. As soon as you've moved on before they've captured the essence of your last point, they now can't begin to process new material until they've decided what to do with the fragment of the last stuff. Do you know what they do? They either decide that the stuff they just missed was unimportant (*It's okay that I didn't get it, it wasn't worth getting anyway*), or, worse, they fill in the missing information with their own to make it make sense (*the graph must have shown that sales weren't falling that fast*).

Filling the Gaps

All the time they're filling in the gaps, of course, they're not following the *new* stuff, and with each new slide they slip further and further behind. Finally, exhausted by running to try to keep up, they collapse and give up. You now have one less of your "following".

If you can deliver each new element that appears on the screen in 10 seconds or less, you'll never have to worry about losing someone to the reading difference bell-curve. At worse, a 50% difference will mean an additional 5 seconds, and that can be managed with simply an additional pause or two. Again, the goal is to get them in the habit of looking to you as the dispenser of the information.

By limiting the time you spend delivering from the screen, you expand your opportunity to bond with the audience. It is only from within this bond that true knowledge transfer takes place. That is the hallmark of all good presentations.

If you can't describe what you are doing
as a process, you don't know what you're doing.
- W. Edwards Deming

Summary

- Audiences are described by bell curves
- People read and process at different rates
- You never have all of their attention
- Your audiences aren't special – they're human
- You've got 10 seconds to make your point

Chapter 5

Stand and Deliver

Where Do You Stand?

Now that you've culled and edited your content down to the point where you know your audience will give you their attention most of the time, where do you stand when you are discussing your slide? (If you're wondering what a discussion about "platform" logistics is doing in a book on presentation design, it's because how you deliver a presentation has everything to do with how you design one. More about this in a moment.)

Of course, as professional presenters ourselves, we know that we are rarely blessed with a perfect room setup in which to present, or even modest control over what we're given. At hotels, especially, it seems that the hiring process for the AV crews usually goes like this:

Interviewer:	Have you ever given a presentation in front of a group before?
Applicant:	Nope
Interviewer:	Have you ever wanted to give a presentation in front of a group before?
Applicant:	Nope
Interviewer:	Have you ever seen a presentation given in front of a group before?
Applicant:	Nope
Interviewer:	Great! You're hired.

And when we're told by the AV guy that we don't need to bring our own projector because they have one built-in, we know we're in trouble, big time.

So when we recommend the best way to position yourself vis-à-vis the screen and the audience, it is with the hope that you can exert at least some influence over the layout of the venue.

Keeping in mind the 75% attention rule, we can always help the process of directing attention by positioning ourselves appropriately depending upon what's on the screen. When new material pops up, it is essential that we stand close to the plane of where we know the audience's attention will be focused -- the plane of the screen. And then if we want to keep everybody in sync, we stay there until we have covered all the information available to see.

You can quickly see how, if we must "clear" the slide before moving away from the Plane of Attention, then the amount of info that comes in must be strictly limited.

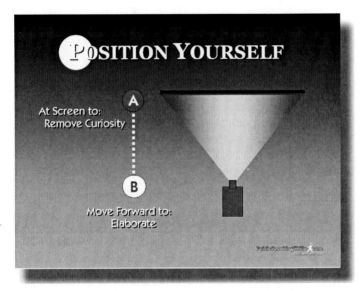

Figure 5.1 When clearing the curiosity about the slide, you make it easier on your audience by remaining in the same plane; to put "meat on the bones", feel free to move forward and let them know that you should now be the center of their attention.

Making Your Bones

Only after you and the audience have both acknowledged the screen info are you allowed to venture forth from the plane and come forward. You come forward, of course, to "put meat on the bones", to expound in detail on what must be nothing more than "talking points" on the screen.

Think, then, of this forward position as where most of the presentation will take place. By separating yourself physically from the screen, you help to further the notion that the screen is there to help, not replace, the presenter. Most of the words in your presentation must originate with you. We know, we know: software like PowerPoint was developed to eliminate the need to remember what we're going to say, and now you want us to memorize stuff again!

It's All in Your Head

Wrong! Good presentations are not about memorization. Far from it. Good presentations occur when you, with your thoughts and organization codified in the on-screen file, are able to "launch" from the screen, and convert your talking points into a conversational discourse about what you know. The less scripted the presentation, the less you'll sound like a...well...*script*, and more like an expert at a lunch table. In fact, that is exactly how you want to envision yourself delivering your presentation - to individuals whom you know quite well around a table over lunch (and perhaps a glass of wine or a bottle of beer). Does that kind of scene make you nervous? Of course not!

Believe it or not, there are many "experts" in the field of presentation skills training that actually encourage people to *memorize* their way to confidence in public speaking. Listen to one such expert, quoted along side us in an article for the online version of USA Today:

"Once you've settled on the verbal and visual content
of your talk, it's time to start rehearsing. Take a small
chunk of the material and practice it out loud 30 to
50 times. Practice it in your throwaway time — in the
shower, on the way to work. Practicing 10 to 20 times
makes you sound rehearsed, but 30 to 50 times makes
you sound natural. By that time you've done it so
much it's like a muscle memory for your throat... You
don't have to think about it."

Can you imagine that? *Fifty* times? How many of you
have the time to take each part of your presentation and
say it fifty times? Why would you want to so thoroughly
memorize a piece that you might only give once, and then
start all over again for the next one? Worse, as good as you
might get with memorizing ninety-five percent of your
presentation, do you know what happens to most people
when they get to the one part they don't remember? They
freak! They freak and then they freeze, and as the fear of
looking foolish builds quickly, their minds lose the ability
to process, *much less recall*, detailed information.

Wouldn't it be better if you had a system that required
no memorization at all? One that simply gave your memory
a shove every few moments and then let you be yourself?
Stay tuned.

The Eyes Have It

In our *Enhancing Your Presentation Skills* course, our firm helps business presenters from all industries learn to both design and deliver presentations that build confidence in the presenter and interest in the audience. A key element of the training involves learning proper eye contact, which requires you to hold contact with one person through the completion of a thought, or roughly anywhere between 3-10 seconds. Most presenters look at one person no more than 1 1/2 seconds at a time, if that, and then only when they're not looking up at the ceiling or down at the floor.

We teach a conversational approach to presenting, because that's the way to maximize comfort between you and the audience. By practicing the techniques we teach, you can deliver to a group of 500 without ever feeling more anxiety than you would discussing your job to friends around a lunch table. Powerful stuff!

Most people like to talk about themselves, about what they do, and about what they know. Your presentations should be like that. Use the screen to keep yourself in a pre-set direction, use it to list all the points you want to be sure to make, but give the presentation itself from the heart. People care somewhat about content, but what moves them to interest is hearing how you *feel* about it. To get across emotion, you want to be conversational.

Reading is NOT fundamental

And putting meat on the bones is exactly what you, the presenter, are there for. Not to read the slide - the audience could do that quite easily for themselves, thank you. In fact, the people who came to hear you speak can read words about 40% faster than you can speak them - 250 words per minute for them vs. 150 wpm for you.

Sound bite: If a sentence works grammatically, it does not work presentationally.

Please do not think that it is OK to have grammatically correct wording on the screen, wording that just begs to be read. When you do, the problem is twofold. You, as the presenter, will not be able to resist reading straight from the screen, because you're conditioned to do that when your brain recognizes a properly structured sentence.

And the audience, also being human, will do exactly the same thing. But their reading takes less time than your speaking, and by getting in their way to be the first to know, you are telling your audience that you really don't care very much about them. It is the equivalent of having a minivan that waits until the last minute to pull out into the road in front of you, and then proceeds to drive 40% slower than the speed limit you were pleasantly exceeding.

Showing Your Best Side

When there is TMI on the screen, especially in the form of sentences, not only does the reading process rob the audience of their precious time, it also leads to breaking the essential bond between audience and presenter that occurs only with constant eye contact. Unable to keep in your head all of the information flashed up on the screen, you are forced, by design, to turn your back to the audience as you read from the screen.

As we demonstrate over and over again in our *Enhancing Your Presentation Skills* class, nothing works more to bind you with the audience than the proper use of eye contact. Our mantra: *If eyes aren't locked, then your jaw must be.* With a visual so complex that it forces you to read from the screen, this all-important component to proper presenting is lost, and attention erodes further.

Absorb, Align, and Address:

The solution, then, is to restrict the volume of information at each exposure to that which can be *absorbed* by both you and the audience in just a few seconds. The proper procedure for achieving transfer of information from the screen to the audience involves a process we call Absorb, Align, and Address.

Absorb

When new information appears on the screen, all eyes will follow it, and at this point it is OK, and desirable, for you to look to the screen also. By doing so, you "give permission" to the audience to get prepared for what's coming next. That's all the screen info should include, too. Just enough information to set the stage for what you are going to discuss. At this point, because you are not looking at any individual in the group, you must be silent.

When you have absorbed the data bite, you can now think for a moment on how to phrase what you want to say to start off. This would not be expounding, but merely filling out the talking points to make a grammatically correct statement.

Align

Once you and your audience have had the opportunity to take in this info, you then need to turn your attention away from the screen, and lock eyes (*align*) with a member of the audience. This is the most difficult part, physically, to perform, as the natural tendency is to begin speaking as soon as you have formulated your statement.

Address

Locked on, you finally can *address* the audience with your version of the talking point.

Again, this address should not be just the words in the bullet point. You may always say more than the line on the screen, but never, never any less. Keep in mind that the group will read everything that's on the screen, so if you put words up there but don't speak to them, you are again insulting your audience: *These words aren't important enough for me to bother with but I wanted to take up your little brains' time just the same.*

Don't Leave 'em Hangin'

Ask yourself how many times has this happened to you: you go to a presentation and see slide after slide with all kinds of footnotes and small type, or graphs with legends and data to which the presenter never refers. You're looking at all the elements on the slide trying to figure out which stuff is most important, and then the presenter never even mentions half the stuff you've read. How does that make you feel? For most people, the first slide that contains more information than the presenter chooses to discuss is the point at which they check out, deciding to figure it all out with the handout. (which, of course, they trash at the first can they see outside the presentation room).

Once learned, the *Absorb, Align and Address* system is a beautiful thing to watch. Slides designed with this system in mind never suffer from TMI, and thus never have too much for you to deal with. Your confidence is high, knowing you're never going to be overwhelmed by the information that appears with the next click of the mouse, and the audience feels this big time. The audience is forced to turn their attention to you, because there's not enough information to allow them to jump to their own conclusions. By the same token, you are now able to direct all of your speaking to the audience and not the screen.

But here's the really fun part: When you follow this simple plan for both design and delivery, almost anyone can look and sound like an expert on their subject, regardless of how much prep time they've put into *rehearsing* the presentation! We prove this in our classes by having participants deliver other participants' presentations that we have edited and revised to comply with the "rules" (next chapter).

Speaking from the Heart

Preferably, off course, you would have a good background in the subject matter so that you can deliver the "meat on the bones" part effectively. But if you know to what the talking points refer, and you also know that no more material than you can deliver in just a few seconds will appear with each click of the mouse, you can actually give a presentation *for the very first time* and sound like you know what you're talking about!

To Build or not to Build

Whenever possible, it is a good idea to employ "builds" when designing slides, because builds, or text animations, provide you with ultimate control of the flow of information. In a subsequent chapter we discuss at length all the rules for incorporating builds properly; when done so, there is almost no opportunity to lose the audience.

Extensive use of builds is generally only a problem if you don't have the right equipment. Your minimum equipment list should include some type of remote mouse, with the more expensive radio-frequency (RF) devices being preferable to infrared systems that require a line-of-sight to the receiver. Otherwise, walking up to a keyboard and striking a key six or more times per slide can be distracting. Professional presenters would never be caught dead without a reliable, freshly charged remote.

If the slide is not designed with builds, you must "clear" each element on the screen before moving out from the plane of the screen to expound on any one point – in other words, to give the presentation. The tendency for most is to address each of the points at length before moving on to the next. But of course that's not what the audience is doing. They are trying to figure out for themselves exactly what each bullet point is about, and won't pay attention to you until they've satisfied their curiosity. So you are forced in this situation to first cover every talking point on the screen, and then back up and fill in each one in turn.

It's OK to have a lot of information on the screen at this point, because you've eliminated the curiosity factor. You can even refer back to a bullet point with a gesture to reinforce their attention to the next topic.

If the content is animated (uses builds), you can take each element and tell the whole story about that point before moving on to the next, or, as with the static slide, briefly clear each point and the go back. Point is, builds provide maximum flexibility, so take advantage of them if you can.

Figure 5.2 Logitech Bluetooth technology mouse sold for about $200 in 2006, and although a truly excellent device, other adequate remotes can bee had for as little as $40.

A Last Pointer:

Any time we go to a presentation and spot a pointer on the podium, we know we're doomed. Pointers worked well for World War II generals to pinpoint bombing targets on blown-up aerial photographs of German industrial facilities; today, their only use as a presentation device is to try to compensate for an overly complicated visual.

The problem with pointers is multifold.

First, having a pointer violates the rule that a good presenter empties his hands and pockets of anything that might be tempting to play with prior to getting anywhere near the platform. This is essential, as your level of anxiety is greatest at the beginning of your presentation, and that is when you are most likely to reach out for and use a crutch. Once employed, it's very difficult to break the habit during your talk. Pointers, given their size, are almost impossible to not play with, whether as a bridge between the hands or as a leg massage tool.

Telescoping pointers are the worst, as the action of stretching and collapsing soon becomes the overbearing focal point of the whole presentation. We've actually witnessed an individual whose nervous energy at the beginning of his presentation was so great that he was able to snap a wooden pointer in half, which of course didn't help his comfort level very much.

Beating it to Death

Second, they violate the rule that you can't engage in any behavior that takes the audiences attention away from the argument that you're there to make. Audiences latch on to the position and direction of the pointer, forever anticipating where it will strike next. And strike it often does, especially if the screen is the pull-down kind that flutters in response to a direct hit. The feel and the sound of this rug-beating can be intoxicating to a presenter, who is often completely unaware of the obnoxious nature of his behavior. However it's used, the pointer becomes the focus, not the content.

Third, and most importantly, a pointer allows the presentation designer to not stop and think about whether the visual could be designed so that the data stands out without having to actively draw attention to it. Are you pointing at one element in the visual because you have more than one concept happening at the same time? In most cases, if you feel the need to use a pointer then you *know* the slide needs to be broken apart into its composite concepts. Separate the components, explain each one, and then show their context in the overall scheme by bringing all the elements together in an additional slide. More about this in the chapter on The Seven Basic Rules: One concept per visual.

Solution:

Depending upon the content you must deliver to your specific audience, we're willing to concede that at some point you will have a legitimate need to "point to" a certain element in your slide. You may have a client who insists on seeing a large amount of data grouped together, or you may need to refer to a specific area of an engineering diagram or even a photograph.

You can add interest or entertainment by showing a "what's wrong with this picture" graphic and then actually pointing it out. Keep in mind that any slide that needs a pointer mechanism to work should be the exception and not the rule.

If, after all your best efforts, you find yourself with a visual that needs specific elements "pointed" to, you can easily solve the pointer problem by clever use of the software rather than old-fashioned hardware.

In this slide where we need to point out what gives "Serif" fonts their name, we call attention to the small extenders at the end of the letters strokes.

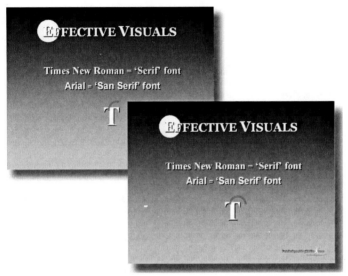

Figure 5.3 Pointers cause more problems than they solve. Instead, use graphics functions in PowerPoint to draw attention to your particular detail.

When the slide first appears, the text is self-evident, but the image of the "T" is not. At this point, we could opt to simply point to what a serif is, but we can be more effective with a simple "drawing" technique.

From the "Drawing" toolbar, we select "Autoshapes", then "Basic Shapes", and from our choice of basic shapes we pick a half-circle. We drag the axis-point of the shape into itself to make the circle less bulky, and then fill it red to stand out. Next, we animate it to "Wipe Left", and when it runs it appears to be "drawn".

Figure 5.4 Here, a simple circle drawn with PowerPoint animation features saves you from having to have the skills of a Hollywood plastic surgeon to keep the laser pointer from jerking the audience into oblivion.

Finally, we make a copy of the half-circle, spin it around, and move it into position to form a full circle. The bottom half we animate to "Wipe Right" automatically after the top half, and to the audience's eye we have dawn a complete circle in one smooth motion.

Review:

As much as we are tempted to show our audiences the breadth and depth of our knowledge, all they are ever looking for is what's in it for them. Furthermore, they won't wait for you to tell them. If it's up on the screen, they will take as much time as they need to figure out what you are trying to say, because as humans they must be "the first to know".

And as much as humans tend to act alike, they all have different abilities, including the speed at which they read. The only possible way to keep the audience on the "same page", and for you to be there with them, is to limit the amount of information that pops up on the screen at any one time. If it takes the average person more than 10 seconds, you risk losing some, if not all, of your audience. And once they've dropped behind, it becomes a real effort on their part (and yours) to get them back.

If detailed content such as statistics or measurements with significant digits is required, the proper place and venue for that information is on a printed document for distribution after the presentation, not on the screen. Thankfully, PowerPoint makes this easy enough to do. Simply create your written presentation with all the information you want to disburse, save it, and then edit that presentation down to the essentials necessary to meet the rules of visual content. Save and present this new file to an audience who will thank you for your brevity, and be inspired to drill down into the written piece for more information.

While Henry Clay's oratorical prowess won him the adulation of much of the House, many less accomplished speakers had difficulty disguising their envy. One notably long-winded speaker once approached Clay and declared that, while Clay's speeches were for the present generation, his own were for posterity.

"And it seems, sir," retorted Clay, "that you are resolved to speak until the arrival of your audience."

Summary

- Don't break their necks – stay in view, make it easy
- Break up your slides, TMI with builds
- No reading: Absorb, Align, and Address
- Say more, never less, than the bullets
- Use graphic solutions to pointers

Chapter 6

The Seven Basic Rules

Follow these rules, and your audience will follow you

Figure 6.1 Most presentations we see today are composed of words and pictures by these two guys. Aren't they dead yet?

Although Salvador Dali is reported to have died in 1989, and William Shakespeare quite a few years prior, they both continue to produce most of the presentations foisted on corporate America today. They evidently often collaborate, with Mr. Shakespeare penning the endless pages of tiny type for which he is noted, while Senor Dali supplies the surrealistic images that can't possibly be understood without the presenter leading a day long discussion on abstract art appreciation.

When Shakespeare put together his first blockbusters, he didn't have Jerry Bruckheimer to wow the crowds with great pyrotechnics, so he had to rely on extended and cleverly convoluted use of the spoken word for most of the entertainment factor. Any of Dali's paintings, or those of other Surrealists, (the school he founded) can provide long periods of entertainment as the observer seeks the hidden meanings in the myriad of abstract images.

But these guys have got to get out of the presentation business!

The Presentation – A Unique Art Form

As tempting as it is for most of us to simply cut and paste our way to a finished presentation from our other MS Office files, the presentation is unfortunately its own unique media. And while the rules of good design transcend many forms of message, there are reasons why the stuff we put up on the screen must conform to rules that don't necessarily apply to other forms of communication.

The most common characteristic among the presentations that our corporate customers send us for review and revision is that they attempt to structure their arguments on the screen in the same way that they do in their handouts. That is, they design their presentations to work as a piece to be read and studied at one's leisure. Unfortunately, what works well when the audience is one individual working at an individual pace and timing doesn't work as soon as the audience is greater than one. People read at their own pace; with a written document they have the ability to skip ahead, go back and re-read, and therefore don't limit themselves to a linear approach.

Take magazines, for example: do you read them front to back or vice versa? Do you read every article straight through, or sometimes start another one when the first one is continued on page 197? Most people have a pretty private relationship with their favorite magazine. Now imagine if the only way you could read a magazine was in concert with a dozen or so other readers. Who would determine the page order? How long would the group spend on one page before moving on to another? Does this sound like fun to you?

Although from time to time Hollywood is able to create a moneymaker from an original script, the overwhelming majority of movies that have ever been made started life as best-selling books. The key to making a great movie from a great book is finding the core elements of the book that tell the story, and of course allowing the visual elements to do as much of the story-telling as possible.

Think about how long it takes you to read a great modern novel, and then think what kind of slaughter a scriptwriter must commit to get the final dialogue and motion in the movie version down to two hours. Most attempts to include more material from the book, and hence produce a final film that runs more than two-and-a-half hours, fail. People simply don't like to sit through three hours of on screen "entertainment", regardless of how much more filling the story may be. Literal rendering of books to film don't work because of volume.

For many of the same reasons, presentations written to also work as handouts become disasters on the screen. Nobody can sit through the same quantity of information from a screen that they can from a written document. Your job as presenter is to take the material you want your audience to really comprehend and put it forth in a way that everyone in the group is digesting it at the same time and is therefore always on the same "wavelength". The rules as set forth in this chapter ensure that with every slide you present, you are not introducing opportunities to let any member of your audience fall off the pace.

So let's look at some basic rules:

1. Favor Right-Brain information
2. K.I.S.S. - Less is More
3. One concept per visual
4. Use proper builds
5. Be colorful - Light on dark
6. Avoid boring fonts
7. Maintain paragraph integrity

Let's take a look at the fundamental reasons behind each of these rules, beginning with the last ones first.

7. Maintain Paragraph Integrity

Size Matters

Perhaps the most common mistake we see in presentations is the seemingly cavalier approach most designers take to font size discipline. And here, Microsoft is very much to blame, for unless you uncheck the default value in the software's Options, PowerPoint will automatically resize your fonts in every slide to fit the text box. Thus we end up with a slide like this:

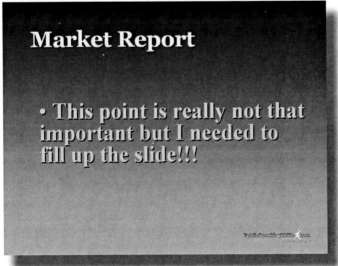

Figure 6.2 We see slides like this all the time…

Figure 6.3...
inevitably followed
by a slide that
looks like this:

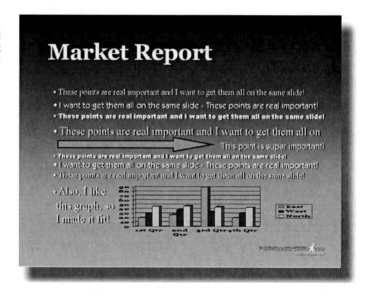

Trouble is, your audience's brain is always trying to apply things it knows against things it doesn't in order to make sense of things in the quickest possible way. It knows, for instance, that a big headline in the morning newspaper means that something really important happened last night; certainly more newsworthy than anything they might find in the small type of the classifieds.

Think about it: if you wake up, walk outside, pick up and unfold your paper and see words in two-inch type splattered across the top, you don't even have to read the words to know that you're in deep doo-doo. Something really *bad* happened last night! On the other hand, if your first glance at the open paper reveals a few columns with normal size type, you know we made it through another night and things are pretty much OK.

If you want to free up your audience's attention to your message, you've got to reduce the amount of energy and bandwidth their brains need for housekeeping functions such as interpreting what the *properties* of the data might mean. Font properties include the style, size, color, and case. In addition, the brain looks for clues such as the location of the data (stuff at the top is probably more important), its proximity to other data (if it's close, it's probably related), and the volume of the data relative to the total volume of information on the screen.

When your audience sees consistencies in font properties from one slide to the next, the amount of brainwork they devote to filtering and interpreting is reduced, and they can devote more resources to digesting your message.

Remember, these things are happening subconsciously, at a level you can't work against (but you can certainly work with). So follow these simple rules:

1. All 1st Level Paragraphs must be the same size in every slide

2. All 2nd Level Paragraphs must be smaller and a different color

3. Don't go beyond the 3rd Level, nor smaller than 20 points

As long as all information of the same importance is of the same size, your audience won't be raising question marks with each slide. You can take this concept one step further by ensuring that all material of the same nature is the same color. If you use a lot of numbers in your bullet points, make them all one color, different from the text. Once your audience recognizes this pattern, they'll spend less time digging through the text to find their figures.

By using font properties to assign importance and relational attributes to your text, the text properties will become visuals. You will thus engage the right brain of your audience, and uptake will be quicker, clearer, and longer lasting.

Don't Jerk Me Around

One final word on words on the page: Never put your audience through "the jerk" as you move from slide to slide. Headlines and the beginning line of text should, in most cases, remain in exactly the same place throughout your presentation. The same rule applies to graphics or anything else that might carry through from one slide to the next. In other words, the only thing that should change between slides is what's new; if the next slide has the same headline and/or graphic, make sure they're in exactly the same place.

The reason we want to do this is that every time a new slide appears, your audience goes through its automatic deciphering process, and has to process all that is new. If the same information appears in a new location, it takes time and effort to process that, but of course nothing new is learned. Wasted brain function.

PowerPoint makes it easy to keep this consistency in two ways. First, if you use **Insert->Duplicate Slide** every time you need a new slide, you will always be starting with a "template" of your last slide, and you can just change the text without changing its properties. Also, unlike other Microsoft Office products, when you copy an object from one slide and paste it into another, it locates it in exactly the same spot as in the slide from which it was copied.

6. Avoid Boring Fonts

Rarely is there a need to use more than two different fonts in any presentation. However, there is a HUGE need to use *any* two fonts other than the PowerPoint defaults Times New Roman and Arial!

It's simply amazing that with all the really bad features that PowerPoint offers designers, the one feature that can easily make your presentation stand out from the crowd, i.e., font control, is so seldom used. Occasionally a presentation comes across our desk that contains 10 or more different fonts, which is a really terrible thing to do, but we'd estimate that 90% of all presentations are done in the Microsoft default fonts.

The problem with using these two fonts is that because everybody else uses them, if yours is the fifth presentation your prospect is seeing that day, pretty soon all the text starts to look the same, and you lose much of your meaning and impact in the process. In fact, we often hear from clients who have to sit through presentations themselves that after a while, they can't remember which vendor said what – it all becomes a big blur. Make sure you're not part of the blur.

Most importantly, fonts can sometimes impart right-brain information just by the way they "shape" the information. As you'll discover in our discussion of Rule Number 1, that can mean everything.

5. Be Colorful

Watch a lot of black-and-white television these days? Although black-and-white works as an art form in many ways, humans tend to like color. Even the old-guard newspapers like the New York Times and the Wall Street Journal finally concluded that to avoid losing readers to more modern media, they had to go to color. Simple fact is that while humans can discern no more than 24 shades of gray, they can see millions of different colors. We've evolved to use our sense of color to survive.

Why, then, do we see so many presentations with black type on white backgrounds? If your answer is that you also have to print your presentation to hand out afterwards (hopefully never *before!*), then you're just as guilty as those who say they need to put *all* the information on the screen because the client insists on seeing *all* the information. The printed presentation that you hand out and the on-screen presentation that you deliver from the platform couldn't be more different in their design requirements. The former, like this book, is meant to be digested at the pace and leisure of an individual; a stand-up presentation is an event that lasts for a specific time and for which you, the leader of this event, must establish a pace for others to follow.

Back to color: If you want to create any interest in the retina, you must use at least two colors; to excite, you need three. Interestingly, for most presentations, using four or more colors tends to distract attention, and we know that's not a good thing.

You want to use color to help maintain a consistency to your visuals. And by limiting your palette, by keeping all the information of a similar kind in similar color, you'll give your audience the consistency they will recognize by about the third slide. This in turn will ease the amount of effort their brains have to exert to understand your message, and their retention will increase.

When you limit the color in your clip-art to the three colors you have chosen for your presentation, you aid retention by making the clip-art's point without diverting attention from your text.

Most clip art is made up of small pieces that are "grouped" together to form the final art. Before you can change colors, you must first select the object, and then from the "Draw" drop-down menu on the Drawing toolbar, choose "Ungroup" (sometimes there are groupings within groups). Now you'll see the clip art is made up of dozens of small pieces. You can delete some elements, and, again from the Drawing toolbar, "fill" the rest with new color.

"In the confrontation between
the stream and the rock,
the stream always wins -
not through strength but by perseverance.
- H. Jackson Brown

4. Use Proper Builds

With all that we preached so far about limiting the amount of information that you want to throw at your audience at any one time, you would think that being able to "build" your on-screen argument one idea at a time would be a good thing. And it is, right up until it becomes too much of a good thing. Without a sense of good design, which as we've seen, in most cases means showing restraint, animations can quickly overwhelm an otherwise well laid-out presentation.

The trick is to bring in your concepts one at a time in ways that don't draw more attention to the build than the concept itself.

We're going to limit the build discussion here as we devote an entire chapter to animations later, and wouldn't want to rain on our own parade. What you'll discover in Chapter 8 are what builds work well (very few) and which ones you'll definitely want to avoid (most). Builds are essential element in turning slides that would otherwise have TMI into ones that audiences can follow every step of the way, but like other elements of good design, a proper build should never announce itself. Rather, a properly animated presentation should simply appear to "happen", without a clue as to why it seems so easy to follow.

The bottom line here is that most slides do one of two things: either all the information appears at once without giving the audience a chance to digest it at a reasonable pace, or the information itself is drowned out by the actions the designer uses to bring it onto the screen. You need to know to find the gentle middle ground that works for both the audience and presenter alike. Again, much more in Chapter 6.

3. One Concept per Visual

Here's another really common problem we see in the majority of business presentations, and the solution flows from the first rule. You can be sure that your visual is not as simple as it needs to be if it contains more than one concept.

In the example slide that follow, we are comparing the difference between graphs and charts in how quickly each conveys the same data. But did you know that upon first glance? Was the concept self-evident? If not, you spent

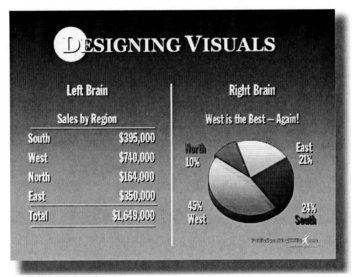

Figure 6.4 When comparing two concepts, you need to introduce each concept on a separate slide, and then create a third when you want to compare.

some time and precious attention span trying to come up with your own interpretation of the visual, didn't you?

You see, when we use this visual in the module on graphs, this is the third slide in the series. The first one contains only the chart. We show it and say that if you need to show data such as sales figures, it helps if you provide good organization, such as a chart. Then we bring up the second slide, and discuss how a graph can get the same message across with less effort on the part of the audience, especially if we title the graph with an action phrase instead of a generic description.

Only after we made those separate points (each *one*

concept), do we then bring them together to introduce the *third* concept, which is the comparison. In this fashion, we raise no question marks, and the audience is always completely in tune.

Remember that as audience members race to be the "first to know", they not only attempt to read everything on the screen to ascertain content, they also attempt to create a hierarchy of importance to the data. When there is more than one concept appearing at the same time, they not only try to figure out the concepts, they try to determine which one deserves most of their attention. This extra time and effort on the part of the audience acts as a drag on presentation flow, and explains why a 45-slide presentation, properly broken down into one concept per, takes less time to present than the same information packed into 15.

Aside: At one class we did for a large international food processor, we were taken aback by the incredible amount of data, graphs and bullet points we found on every one of the twelve participants' slides. As we got into the design module and they started to see why our rules work, we began to notice some resistance to our instructions to break their slides down into individual concepts.

Finally, one of the participants raised her hand and said, "We all can see exactly what we should do now, but if we follow your rules we won't be able to give our whole report". When we reiterated that it would indeed take less time to deliver with more slides, she replied, "That's great – except our presentations are only allowed to be 12 slides long!"

Evidently someone way up the food chain (as it were) at one point grew tired of sitting through the company's typically convoluted presentations, and sent down an edict that forevermore throughout the kingdom all presentations would be reigned in to a royal length of twelve slides. After several letters to their management that we wrote on behalf of our beleaguered participants failed to move them from their perch, we finally convinced them to let us put on a demonstration.

After a very eloquent employee gave her budget proposal, designed with the 12-slide ordinance, to a group of superiors in product development and finance, we got up and gave the same one. Only of course ours ran to 33 slides, and we knew nothing about either their budget or product development processes.
It was quite entertaining to see the slack in their

collective jaws as we delivered the material sounding like the polished experts we obviously were not, and completed the delivery of the same data in 9 minutes verses her 13. Two weeks later we were copied on an email to all employees explaining that there had been some confusion about the permitted length of company presentations.

The memo stated that, of course, the limit of 12 still applied, but that was (always) meant to have referred to the number of minutes, not slides! Sometime later we learned that our little demonstration had immediately shaken up the human resources bureaucracy, but it had taken them two weeks to come up with a memo that covered everybody's tracks!

Although the point in this example might have been completely clear to you from the beginning, can you imagine what happens when you show a slide that has three or four concepts?

"Consider how hard it is to change yourself
and you'll understand what little chance you have
in trying to change others."
- Jacob M. Braude

2. Less is More

Although anybody born before the last millennium knows what this means, it's a concept that doesn't make it into many presentations. What we see most often is an attempt by the presentation designer to let the world know just how deep and broad his knowledge of the particular subject is.

Speechwriter and columnist Peggy Noonan, who is also an expert in public speaking, is fond of reminding us that to draw in an audience, it's much more about your passion toward a subject than your knowledge. One of her oft-quoted sentiments (which she rightfully attributes to someone else) is:

"They won't care how much you know until they know how much you care."

And that pretty much sums up the reason to ask yourself whether you really need to add that extra bullet point, that 12-point type graph, or that spreadsheet to your current slide. These days, facts are easy to come by. You want to find some data about an obscure subject? Simple – just go to the Internet. And because facts are so easy to come by, people are less and less impressed by facts alone. Putting a bunch of facts on a slide doesn't impress too many people today.

Unless you're Indiana Jones giving a first-hand account of your recent personal findings in Egypt or Africa, thousands of people are not likely to turn out to hear you speak about your latest expedition and discoveries. Today, people get can all the facts they want cheaply and conveniently. The reason they would come to hear you speak would be to witness the passion you exude about the stuff you know.

Here's the thing about keeping it simple: Einstein once said that *"an explanation should be as simple as possible, but no simpler"*. Some presenters familiar with the Keep-it-Simple rule tend to make the whole presentation not just simple but simple-minded. But as Edward Tufte says, don't assume that your audience has gotten dumber just to come hear you speak. When we talk about simple, we're referring to nothing more than the design of individual slides.

You may be giving a presentation on the latest successful techniques in human cloning, and that's not likely to lend itself to an 8th grade reading level. But even the most intricate subjects of scientific or engineering presentations have to be designed so that when the slide appears, most people get it right away.

Eliminating Question Marks

Your job as presentation designer is to create an interactive document that 1) supports the ideas, concepts, or arguments you need to put forth, and 2) keys the audience to what you're going to talk about just before you fulfill your role in the process, which is to *deliver the presentation*. And that's the rub: the presentation is not what's on the screen. And neither is the presentation what comes out of the presenter's mouth. The presentation is actually only what takes place in the mind of the listener. And it takes place there because you are firing up their imaginations, memories and emotions. It takes a human to do that, and that is why they have come to your presentation – to be spoon fed and inspired by an expert.

The temptation with PowerPoint is to let the software and the hardware do all the work, allowing you to be just a casual moderator of the whole event. Yet when we think that we can simply put everything we want them to know on the screen and let the audience read it themselves, we insult them with bad, lazy design.

We've written at length about the need to limit the *amount* of information that arrives on the screen at any one time, but it's important to also limit the *complexity* of that information. You know by now that audience members will not wait for you to explain what the slide is all about, that they will do whatever they must be the first-to-know. Thus to keep them in your fold you must look really hard at every slide with an eye to eliminating the question marks that light up over their heads as each new visual appears:

Where am I?

Where do I Begin?

What's Most Important?

Figure 6.5 When a slide hits the screen, people have a need to be the first to know – so immediately question marks spring up. Your job is to eliminate as many question marks as possible – which you can with proper design.

These are the questions that most slides provoke, and the more question marks your slides raise, the more wave lengths you have to deal with, and the less cohesion you have in your audience. In fact, the problem with introducing question marks at all is that they breed rather rapidly.

When an audience member is provoked into asking a question *in his own mind* by a confusing element in your slide, it often sets in motion a cascade of questions that quickly overtake the amount of RAM available for uptake of your actual message. When you send an audience member off on a search for understanding, you never know where their mind will take them – except to know that it's probably not to your desired destination.

Self-Evident v. Self-Explanatory

Of course it's not possible or even desirable that *everything* that appears is immediately clear to the entire audience. You do need a few surprises once in a while to shake them up and keep them guessing. And, as the audience is there to learn something new from you, the expert, you wouldn't be giving a very memorable presentation if everybody already knew and understood everything you were there to talk to them about.

What you bring up on the screen needs to *prepare*

them for what you're going to explain, and not attempt to be the explanation itself. Once again, it's not about the screen!!! What you really want to strive for in your design is for items to be self-evident. The visual should, in the literal sense, speak for itself. It should not raise questions that start audience members off on their own voyages of self-discovery.

If you can't make your visual self-evident, try for the next best, *self-explanatory*. A self-explanatory visual at least contains the explanation within the slide, so that if at first question mark flags are flown, they are quickly lowered. A good example of self-explanatory would be a graph with a legend that is large, clear and tied directly into the design of the graph, rather than in a hard-to-read adjacent table. A self-*evident* graph would not need a legend at all. (There's more to come on graphs in their own subsequent chapter.)

To review, your presentation should be as simple as possible, but with respect for the intelligence of your audience, no simpler. Because a well-designed presentation takes place in the minds of the audience, it's not what's up on the screen that determines how good your presentation is, its how passionately you transfer that information to your listeners. And you can't do that really well unless you keep the focus on you and not the screen. To keep the focus on you, you have to limit the amount of information on the screen, and Keep It Simple, Sweetheart.

Less is More

A full-page ad in the Wall Street Journal sells for around $100,000. If you were spending that kind of money, would you devote the vast majority of that real estate to empty space?

Do they enjoy wasting their clients' money? Is there a good reason to devote so much of an ad to "white space"? Well, the answer is that in many cases, when trying to make a strong impression, less is often more. In other words, the less ink spent on messages that might divert attention from the main one, the more impact the main message has.

When designing your slides (or for that matter your whole presentation), keep in mind that not only are audience attention spans short, their retention is painfully low, too.

When one of the major business seminar companies out of Shawnee Mission, Kansas, did a six-month long survey of thousands of attendees to their one-day programs, they realized that their typical adult learner retained only 10% of what she had learned less than a week before!

Your mission, then, is to determine not only if the piece

Figure 6.6
Advertisers aren't
wasting their money
when they purchase
full-page ads and
then don't fill them
up with pitches for
their product. Often,
Less is More.

of information you feel you simply *must* include on your slide is relevant, but also whether it will have staying power in the mind of your listener. Is it "need-to-know", or only "nice-to-know"? Nice-to-know info makes for good talking matter to back up your main point, but only need-to-know material should ever appear on the screen.

The Power of White Space

You need to resist the urge to show and tell more, and instead, seize the power of white space.

Most untrained presentation designers try to cram too much information or too many design elements into a slide, preventing the audience from understanding and absorbing their main message.

This rule is essential for graphs or charts. We often see pie charts come across our review desk with over a dozen slices, many so small they need to be annotated with lines and arrows far from the graph itself.

Do you really think anyone will remember all 25 competing products in your market and their percentage share? Might be good information for a handout, but in a presentation few people can absorb more than six elements in any graph. You make your point much more effectively when you limit your displayed data to the stuff the audience is likely to remember:

than when you try to tell them everything:

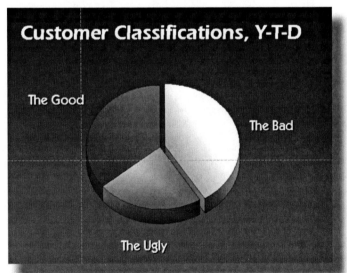

Figure 6.7 In the "low resolution" world of computer screens, there are severe limitations to how many data points you can represent in any graph or chart.

Figure 6.8 Rarely does your audience need to see all the data *on the screen* to understand you main conclusion. Details like those above are suitable for the handout you'll distribute *after* your talk.

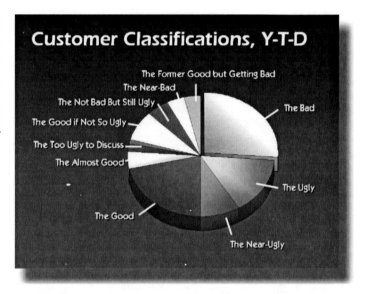

By restricting the quality of "screen-ink", as Dr. Tufte likes to call it, to only the best, you don't dilute the images burned into your listener's retina memory. Less information becomes more retention of the stuff you really want them to go home with.

Aside: For those bean-counter types reading this, I already hear your saying, "But our audiences require *all* the data – they insist on seeing every slice". Well, for those times when that really is true, PowerPoint actually provides a pretty nifty solution: hyperlinks. We recommend that for every slide about which someone might ask to see more detail, you have two slides. The simple version is the one that everyone sees, and if nobody needs to know more, your presentation is that much more crisp and concise. But just in case you're called on the carpet for more information, you have the detailed, complicated one somewhere at the end of your presentation, connected to the main slide with a hyperlink.

The simple graph itself can serve as the object containing the hyperlink, and the complicated graph as the return path. If the more detailed graph is positioned in the slide exactly when the first one is, it will really knock them for a loop when you "expand" your graph on command, and then shrink it again when you're done. Pulling this trick a couple of times will often stop the calls for more detail, especially if they come from a boss who's only trying to see if you've done your homework. (More on hyperlinks in Chapter 7)

The $20 Axiom

Everybody likes to save time and money, don't they? With this axiom, you can start thinking of designing presentations from a frugal point of view.

We like to say that talk is cheap, but don't think of words you put in your slides as free, just because a meter doesn't go click with every one you slap on the screen. Instead, think of words as being precious, if not priceless. We suggest that you think of each word as being worth twenty dollars.

Why twenty bucks? Well, maybe because in the new millennium it doesn't mean as much to know "the value of *a* dollar" as it once did. The point is, every word you include in your slide has a significant value – one that costs you when you use it and rewards your frugality when you find a way to save one.

You may have heard that Mark Twain would quip that the more time he had to write a speech, the less he would charge. His most expensive speech (and he did charge for speaking – his only source of income for most of his life) was an impromptu one. He needed weeks to prepare one that sounded genuinely spontaneous.

If you know that every word you use will cost you twenty dollars, and consequently every one you edit out will put twenty dollars in your pocket, you'll likely spend more time deciding how you can say what you need to say in the most concise way. Just as even the best actors need strong directors, the best presentation writers need editors. If you can't afford to pay one (and who can?), then you must be your own. But edit you must! Cut! Chop! Reword! The typical slide we see has at least 50% more verbiage than necessary to get the point across.

And think of it this way, too: don't let the screen steal your thunder. If you've got something really great to say, don't share it with the screen. Share your wisdom with your audience after you've "cleared" the bullet point and you have the chance to step away from the screen and become conversational.

If you feel there's value in what you have to say, assign a value to the words you use on the screen, and be frugal.

CREATIVITY
*You're only given
a little spark of madness.
You mustn't lose it.*
- Robin Williams

Finally, in case we haven't mentioned it before:

1. Favor Right-Brain Information

When you pick up a magazine and leaf through it, what grabs your attention? It's not the text of the articles, is it? If you're a normal human, your eye is automatically attracted to the pictures or the graphics. To understand, let's drop back for a moment and review what many of you know about the old right brain, left-brain thing.

We humans have evolved with two different ways to deal with stimuli from the outside world so that we can react to it in the way most likely to keep us alive. It's a pretty neat trick if you think about it. Our right brain reacts to input such as colors, graphics, shapes and patterns instantly, without stopping to process the information first. In some cases, our hardwiring will cause input from the optic nerve to trigger involuntary use of a large muscle group, such as your legs.

Case in point: You and your friend are in the jungle, traversing a valley on an 200-foot long Indiana Jones-type bridge. One hundred feet below, a river scours over huge and rapids. All of a sudden, up from under the bridge slithers this huge, 20-foot long snake. Big enough to swallow you whole. From a few eons ago, your genes have held an image of this snake, and it's not a good image. It's yellow and orange, and has these red spots down its back. It opens up it jaws and you see blood on its teeth from its last grab. What do you do?

Well, many people say, "Run!", but the problem is snakes get faster as they get bigger, and a human can't outrun a 20-foot snake – hence those pictures of Anacondas with whole animals in their bellies. So what do you do?

Well, you don't stop and try to remember its Latin genus name – you jump. Or, rather, your hamstrings retract and then your quadriceps extend, sending you into the stream. You don't like falling or getting wet, but without asking, your brain decides it prefers living, and over you go.

Your right brain just took charge. You see, your right brain, reacting and responding to the type of information it understands, namely shapes and colors and patterns, sees the snake and determines that its staring at Certain Death. It then checks out the surroundings, sees the water a hundred feet below, and concludes that a quick vertical exit would result in Probable Injury. It then takes a millisecond or so balancing the prospect of Certain Death vs. Probable Injury and says, "Hmmmmmmmmmmmm".

You are wet, bruised and confused, but alive!

The Other Side

Now let's look at a similar scenario from your left brain's point of view. You're survived the fall into the stream, and have climbed back up the cliff. You're not a happy camper, and you still have to walk across the same bridge.

This time, halfway across, your friend yells out, "Snake! Jump! Snake! Jump!". "Not again!" you think, only this time, with the snake not in your field of view, you find yourself still on the bridge. No auto-maneuver.

Then you remember that your friend, although fond of hiking, has a deathly fear of snakes, all snakes, and the last time you went hiking, she shrieked at the site of a garter snake, in fact a *baby* garter snake. This time you decide to see for yourself if you're dealing with a threat worth getting wet all over again.

Your left-brain has actually stopped to *process* the input before acting on it. The input in this case was not a visual, but rather speech, similar to text and therefore subject to *interpretation* by your brain's logic center. After all, another jump into the ravine might have gotten you hurt, and before doing that, your left-brain had to know whether its working with good information. Left-brain information, such as speech or text or numbers or sequences, is not immediately acted upon as right-brain information is. Rather, it is first filtered and processed.

And that's why we have two different hemispheres.

The result of this process in less-than-life-threatening situations is that although we absorb colors and patterns and graphics instantly and not analytically, when presented with speech, text or numbers, we pause to analyze the data before storing or reacting to it. We have filters on the left side, and not everything gets through.

So to entice the brain to instantly absorb and then retain words, it's necessary to trick the hemisphere into thinking it's dealing with right-brain type stuff. We do that by turning the words into music, which the right brain discerns as a pattern. Right brains like patterns. That's why, for instance, advertisers like jingles; jingles work so well because we don't first process the info before absorbing it. Similarly, stories, concocted properly, can also be absorbed as pattern.

A Bullet to the Head

When you think about the last dozen or so presentations you've had to sit through, what did they mainly consist of? Were there mostly pictures, graphs, and images, or ten to twenty slides of bullet points? If you can't remember much from these last dozen productions, they were probably mostly bullet points. Left-brain filters are also the gatekeepers to short-term memory, and for any input to make it into long-term memory, it must first etch into the short-term matter.

Repeat: Use Pictures, Graphs, & Images

Ideally, what you want to do is design slides that reach out to both sides of the brain. That's where artwork often can work to your advantage.

Figure 6.9 In this slide, the concept is that a visual should not contain more than six lines of text, with no more than six words per line. The picture of the 6 x 6 creates a memory anchor in the brain to which to attach the concept. We also create a self-evident pattern with the words for even more dual-hemisphere absorption.

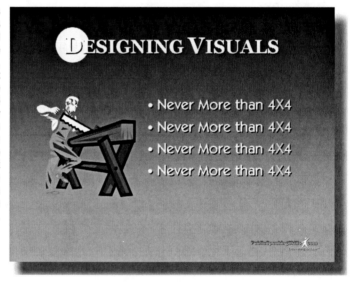

*"What we see depends mainly
on what we look for."*

- John Lubbock

Summary

- Favor Right-Brain information
- K.I.S.S. - Less is More
- One concept per visual
- Use proper builds
- Be colorful - Light on dark
- Avoid boring fonts
- Maintain paragraph integrity

Chapter 7

Creating Effective Content

Stating your case so that your
audience responds

Taking the Active Approach
First thought: to whom are you speaking?

Ken Haemer, a human resource professional with AT&T, once said, *"Designing a presentation without an audience in mind is like writing a love letter and then addressing it to* To Whom it May Concern."

So before we talk about creating effective content, it's important to remember that you can't create content with true meaning for your audience before you make a thorough analysis of exactly who that audience is. Typical questions we need to know are:

What do you have in common with them?

How knowledgeable is the audience about the subject?

Are they there because they want to or because they have to?

What expectations might they have?

What have they been told about you?

What is their profession or occupation?

What's their level of experience and education?

What are some of the toughest questions you might expect?

How many others will have spoken before you?

About what?

How will the audience view you: 'one of us', 'outsider', etc.?

Will the audience be subordinates or superiors?

Will they be well-wishers, or nay-sayers?

Is this presentation motivational, informational, or other?

Why should your audience listen to what you have to say?

Of course, regardless of how well we do our homework, it's usually never possible to anticipate the entire makeup of our audience. Audience analysis is more art than science, and in most cases all we can really do is shoot for the middle and hope for the best.

There is a way to construct computer-based presentations that anticipates the need to change content on-the-fly, and we'll explore that technique at the end of this chapter. The point we want to emphasize here is that although you might not know all you'd like to about the people to whom you will present, the more of those audience analysis questions you can answer, the more likely your chances for success.

WII-FM

Our last concept here refers to the most widely listened-to radio station in the world, whose call letters are an acronym for "What's In It For Me?" When you're giving your presentation, you need to understand that it's the only wavelength your audience is tuned to.

Unfortunately, when most people design a presentation, they start by listing all the things they know about the topic, and then try to arrange those things in some kind of order. If the order makes sense, they feel that they have accomplished their goal. In other words, their orientation is about what they know. This is one reason that most presentations are so convoluted; presenters are so concerned that audiences will judge them on the extent of their knowledge, that they put everything they know on the screen!

Stop for a moment and think about the last time you were in the market for a big-ticket product, such as a an automobile or consumer appliance. When you walked into the store and began your dance with the salesperson, what about the product did the salesperson emphasize? If the salesperson was average, he probably launched into a full-blown presentation of all the nifty new features of the product, and touted a litany of numbers and performance figures.

If the salesperson was a pro, however, he first would have asked you a series of questions about your needs, letting you know that he cared about matching you up with the right product. And then instead of focusing on the products *features*, he would have touted the *benefits* that those features would provide to you.

If you think of your audiences as prospective buyers of your ideas, you will begin to think more in terms of what the benefits of your ideas are, and not just the features. A properly designed presentation will also focus on what's important to the audience. After all, it's not about you – it's about them.

The 'Me' Factor

Speaking of you, think about this: How many presentations have you attended that started off with the presenter talking about him or her self?

"Hi, my name is Bob Jones. I've been with my firm for over seven years now and in this industry for almost fifteen. I'm head of research now, but before that I spent three years in product development, and two more in marketing. I have some really great ideas that I'll share with you later, and I'm looking forward to spending the next couple of hours with you here today."

Gee, Bob, that's great. But why the hell are *we* here? Audiences don't care what you can do; they care about what you can do for *them*. An approach based on providing the features and benefits of your being there today would do a much better job of engaging the Audience from the get-go.

"Good morning, I'm Bob Jones. I'm here today because I've been working in this industry for fifteen years [a feature of Bob's], *and I thus have the experience to save you literally months of research* [a definite benefit]. *What's more, you can stop worrying about trying to keep up with all the government regulations that affect our business* [benefit], *because I literally wrote the book when I led a volunteer government task force last year* [feature]."

The same rule applies to how you speak about your

firm. Lecturing your audience about your firm's history since the turn of the century or showing an organizational chart of all the key players will not engender interest. What can history, or a group of names, titles, and report-to paths do for them?

For every element you put on your slide, and for the content of your presentation, literally try to discern it from the audience's point of view. Look at the slide as a participant, and ask yourself, "What's in it for me?" If you can't find a benefit, rest assured they won't either.

Creating Order

Now that we know to whom we will be presenting, it's important to make it clear that we care enough about them to have spent the time to tailor our content to their particular needs and abilities to learn.

And we do that, first of all, by making it easy for them to understand the basis and flow of our argument. To help your audience gather a sense of where you're going, assign some type of order to your speaking points. This order might be:

• Chronological
• Alphabetical
• Numeric
• Order of Importance

By alerting the audience to the type of order you'll be using, you help their comprehension in two ways: 1) you prepare them for the quantity of information they will have to digest, and 2) you free them from confusion over where you're going next.

For instance, if you start off by saying, *"Today we have five major goals that must be met this quarter"*, the audience knows how much memory it must set aside for the upcoming information. If you announce that you're going to establish a timeline for an upcoming project, the audience can work with a simple calendar in their minds to know where to place the tasks. This is a classic way of working with our natural learning process of always wanting to apply what we know (the orderly passage of time) to something we don't (the content of your presentation).

And obviously if you begin by saying you're going to discuss problems or tasks in the order of their importance, you free up brain power to consider the concepts without their having to discern for themselves just how relatively important your current concept is.

Notice here that we talk about establishing an *order*, rather than an *agenda*. We shy away from the agenda concept not because we don't think you should have one, but rather because agenda *slides* are typically overused crutches that presentation designers rely on to frame their presentations. How many times have you had to sit through a presentation that begins with:

"Good Morning, my name is Bob, and here's what we're going to talk about today. First, we'll start with the introduction, which is where we are now, and then after the introduction we'll talk about the history of our company. Then we'll take a look at where we are now, and what's new in product development. That should take us up to the 10:30 break. After the break, we'll discuss..."

Most audiences will tune the presenter out before he gets to describe how long the afternoon break will be. Never count on arousing your audience with a format they've suffered through dozens of times before. For content to be effective, it first of all must be original.

It's about Them

The real problem with agendas is they are presenter-based, rather than audience-based. An agenda is about how you are going to spend *your* time; an ordered presentation is about helping the audience know what's important and where you're going – in other words, it's about *them*.

We see the same thing with opening slides that are all about the company's history or maybe its products, rather than about the solutions those products can provide for the audience. It is essential you gain your audience's attention and interest right out of the gate. You do that by having content that addresses their interests, not with "impressive" data about your company.

So instead of having an opening like this:

Figure 7.1
Unfortunately, nobody cares about either you or your company, much less its history, until you have given them a good reason to. Keep all the great stuff about yourself until after you've demonstrated all the great things you can do for *them*.

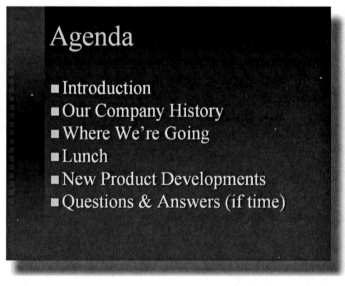

You will more likely stir interest with one like this:

Our Top 5 Goals

Know You
Learn your Vision
Analyze your Strengths
Discover Areas to Improve
Recommend a Successful Solution

Figure 7.2 Next time, try starting off by signaling that you care more about their needs than about the solutions you'd like to sell.

The fact of the matter is that audiences really don't give a darn about you or your company until they've been shown what you can do to make their lives easier, more comfortable, free of fear or full of profit.

Only after you've established what problem you can solve will listeners be receptive as to why your company should be the one they choose to solve the problem. People want to hear about themselves. Accommodate them, and you will keep their attention.

The Incredible Journey

Of course, to help you decide just what order you should use, it helps to know where you plan to go. Before you put together all the "facts" you want your audience to know, ask yourself what you want your audience to do at the end of your presentation. Your question should sound something like this:

When I'm finished, my audience will _____

- Buy my product
- Ask for more information
- Approve my Recommendation
- Ask for another Meeting
- Ask for a Proposal

Once you know what sort of response you want, you can build an order to your concepts that are tuned to deliver that response. Think of your presentation as a journey – a journey in which you are leading a group of explorers. You know what you want them to discover, you know where you are going, how long the journey should be, and its destination.

Leadership is the capacity to translate vision into reality."
- Warren G. Bennis

Statistics

When using statistics to make your case, there are a few ways you can make them less "cold" and thus more capable of generating an emotional response.

First, as in everything else we've discussed here, determine how necessary it is to display numbers out to their least significant digit. Will you be misrepresenting if instead of saying that sales increased by 9.873 % last year, you say that sales increased by darn near 10%?

Second, try to create a picture with your numbers, and put them in perspective. You could say that increasing our nations' fuel economy by 1% would save a billion barrels of oil every year, but who can actually envision a billion barrels, or a billion anything else for that matter. We don't count billions on an everyday basis, so we have no perspective.

Instead, you could say that increasing fuel economy by 1% would save enough fuel to power 800,000 SUV's each and every year, or provide free gasoline for a year for every vehicle in Philadelphia.

Third, by putting statistics in human terms, your audience will relate to the data on a more emotional level, rather than putting up those filters as they do will all straight left-brain input.

Making an argument for increasing foreign aid based on historical trends will excite few people. Showing how for every $10 we send in food aid to East Africa each year, one family loses one less child to starvation, sends a message that even the heartless in your audience can't escape.

Speak to Them

Finally, don't dilute your message by talking about people in general. To arouse the interest and attention of your audience, speak to them in the second person – tell them how they will be affected.

Don't say: *"Participants will benefit…"*
Do say: *"As a participant, you will benefit…"*

Don't say: *"40% of people will suffer from heart disease…"*
Do say: *40% of you will contract heart disease …"*

Don't say: *"The five things I'll discuss today are…"*
Do say: *Five things you will learn today are …"*

Similarly, don't weaken your argument by punting; let them know how strongly you believe in what you're telling them. For instance:

Don't say: *"I think you will agree that..."*

Do say: *"I'm certain you'll agree that ..."*

Don't say: *"I hope you will consider..."*

Do say: *"I strongly recommend that, starting today, you consider ..."*

Hyperlinks: Making Content Relevant

As much as you follow all the rules to make your content effective, it's a rare event that everything works in your favor. You don't always know who will make up your final audience, or how long you will actually have to present. Until recently, your typical linear presentation didn't always play well when either one of these factors changes at the last minute.

But now we have hyperlinks, and designing all of your presentations to take advantage of this new flexibility should be a prime goal. Hyperlinks allow you to, in effect, reconstruct your presentation on the fly based on any changes in the presentation environment. Through designing-by-hyperlink, you can build a complete library of presentation modules that are easier to edit and manage than one long, linear, all-inclusive file.

Make it easy on yourself

Many presentation experts tell you to always start with an outline of your presentation before you commit any of your concepts to slides. This helps you to keep to a predetermined order, which is easier for both you and your audience to follow. The problem with this approach is that it tends to constrict spontaneous thinking; many people come up with great ideas for a slide at inconvenient times. If you have to work with an all-encompassing outline to decide where this new concept might best fit, it can be difficult. But if your total presentation were really a collection of many small, well compartmentalized units, each of a specific topic, adding a slide would be a simple matter of opening a small file and inserting it somewhere between perhaps 10 slides rather than 100.

Hyperlink allows you to create a presentation that can be structured very much like a web site. You can have a "home" slide that shows the different "pages" you can go to, and even let your audience decide what direction the presentation will take. Using copies of that same home slide, you can insert them at the end of each module so you can always return to a known spot. It's not very complicated to set-up, and it gives you both flexibility and the appearance of professionalism, especially if you have to change your presentation at the last minute and you don't want the audience to know it.

The Object of your Desire

In PowerPoint, any object – text box, graphic, AutoShape, WordArt, etc. – can be made into a clickable Hyperlink simply by selecting it, right-clicking, and choosing Action Settings. From there, choose On Mouse Click, and then see the various things you can do. Not only can you navigate to specific slides in your open presentation, you can launch brand new ones.

So in any one slide you can create the option to branch to several different slides – your choices for creating content on the fly are literally unlimited. Of course, it's a good idea to have a disciplined approach to navigation here. You always want to include a well-designed path back from wherever you just jumped. Again, with a Home slide structure, you're only one click away from knowing where you are.

Hint: From the Master Slide, assign a "Home Slide Return" hyperlink to your logo.

To add a Hyperlink to any Object such as text, clip art, AutoShape, etc.:

- Select (or Create) Object
- Right Click, Click 'Action Settings'
- On 'Mouse Click' tab, Select 'Hyperlink'
- Choose Slide or Other File

Experiment: Take your last presentation, break it down into at least three specific modules, and create a Home Slide and link to each module.

Telling Tales

Finally, nothing helps get your audience to listen to you more than when you tell stories. Long before we had presentation technology, long before we had even books or paper and pen, we learned news and history through the oral medium of stories. As a child you learned through stories. The tenets of most major religions are told through stories.

And if you pick up a copy of *The Wall Street Journal*, a fairly respected business publication, you will note that the left-hand, center, and often the right-hand columns all begin not with a Who-What-Where-When journalism approach, but rather in the form of stories:

"In the early days of the first Bush administration, when Jeff Bezos was just a year out of college and earning $225 a week as clerk, the soon-to-be multi-millionaire entrepreneur had an idea...."

Stories allow you to put that all-important human touch to your argument. Sometimes, with business presentations, it may seem difficult to decide how to put something as dull as the chemical ingredients of the new compound you're working on into a story. But for most projects, there's a timeline – a past and a future – and a character – perhaps you – working to complete a task or solve a problem. All stories have three elements:

+ A Character

+ A Problem

+ Movement toward a Solution

Hence the classic:

"Boy meets Girl" – the characters

"Boy loses Girl" – the problem

"Boy gets Girl back" – the plot of the movie

Find every opportunity you can to fit the facts of your case into the framework of a story. People are intrigued by other people, challenged by a problem, and engaged throughout a timeline that shows movement toward solving that problem. Raise their curiosity, and they'll want to be the *first to know* the ending!

Summary

- As thoroughly as possible, know to whom you speak
- You? No, it's about them
- Begin at the end – know what you want from them
- Give facts and statistics human relevancy
- Don't dump data – tell stories!

Chapter 8

Animations & Transitions

Controlling the flow of information

Why Animate?

To begin, by animation we simply mean to control the way and order in which an object appears on the screen. PowerPoint blesses us with 144 different ways to "introduce" text or graphics, almost all of which are major detractors from the presentation itself. In this chapter, we'll examine which of these "special effects" work to enhance the presentation process, and which, like the default effect FLY, have helped to create the disastrous level of presentation quality that we take for granted in business today.

Words vs. Graphics

Birds, airplanes, and Frisbees all fly. Words don't. With PowerPoint, you can attach the same special effects to text as you can to any other object, no matter how inappropriate. So where it might be very fitting to have a clip-art airplane fly across the screen, the worst animation you can apply to a group of words is the one most people use.

Here's the problem: as we learned earlier, people in your audience are human, and are genetically engineered to want to be the first to know. They can't wait for you to tell them, and if their vision is captured by a light source, they can't avoid trying to discern its meaning or importance, instantly. When a group of words goes flying across the screen, even though the moving text is very difficult to read, the audience can't help but try to read the text before it stops. But after even just a few lines of flying text, which drag the brain from somewhere off screen and then whack it with the abrupt stop at the end, comprehension is quickly overwhelmed by the energy needed to keep up with the action.

Add to that the lovely sound of screeching brakes or broken glass, the two most used sound effects, and you have an audience whose main focus is on when the presentation will end (and the pain will stop!).

And though FLY is a really, really bad way to introduce text, there are others capable of worse damage. SWIVEL (rhymes with drivel) demands that you sit through three complete revolutions of the text you want to read before it settles down to let you do so. CRAWL is useful if you want to prolong the agony of FLY, as it creates the same effect, only at half the speed. Bring in your text with CHECKERBOARD, and you can draw real tears in just three slides!

The fun really begins when you mix up the different variations PowerPoint empowers you with, such as having the first line fly in from the left, the next from bottom-right, a couple more from the top, all the while adding a different sound effect to each direction of flight.

Proper use of animation is quite rare in the thousands of slides we see each year. We generally see either no animation at all, especially in slides with too many lines of text in the first place, or we see mind-numbing overuse bordering on abuse. So what's a designer to do?

The Final Four

To use animations properly, you first need to remember that words and graphics create different responses in the audience's brain, and work with that reality.

As with everything else you now know about design, the best animations are the simplest. For those of you who have made the move to the latest version of PowerPoint, you finally have one animation that you should consider above the rest: FADE.

The fade has been around since Cecil B. DeMille times (let's say the 1920's), and nobody putting text on a big screen has been able to improve on it much since. If you have it, use it. It is *the* most gracious of the animations, as it is the gentlest. Whether or not it is worth your "upgrading" to the latest version is your decision – the program has actually come to require more labor with each new iteration, so you have to make a real cost/benefit decision here.

Otherwise, for text, only four of the available build animations are appropriate:

1. Wipe (Up, Down, Right, & Left)

2. Random Bars (Horizontal & Vertical)

3. Dissolve

4. Appear

What these effects have in common is a) a gentle motion, and b) they don't move the text as they work; in other words, the text itself remains static, causing no violence to the eye or brain. DISSOLVE would work better if the grain were less coarse. For this reason, we often use RANDOM BARS Vertical, and mix in a little Horizontal every now and then to change things up. In the same manner, we will use APPEAR every once in a while in conjunction with the other two.

The rule is that you want to use at least two different animations for your text, but not more than three. If you use one animation 60% of the time, another 30%, and a third 10%, your presentation will remain consistent yet not entirely predictable. Those percentages refer to the times you *do* animate. Animation is definitely not required, or encouraged, for every slide.

If your concept is self-evident (or the next-best, self-explanatory) with all of your text appearing at once with the change-of-slide, by all means do not animate it. Animation builds are there to control the flow of information in a way that provides maximum clarity. A very well designed slide often needs no restrictions; indeed, a very strong presenter delivering well-edited material can often be as effective with the old slides or overheads.

But are you that good? Most of us are not, which is why builds are a good thing. Just remember, it's about the presentation, not about the effects.

The Graphic Difference

With graphics, we have a few more options. While still true that the best animations are the simplest because graphics are processed by the right-brain, we don't have the same processing problems when the image is not static.

For objects other than text, these build animations are appropriate:

1. Wipe (in the appropriate direction)

2. Split (Horizontal & Vertical, In & Out)

3. Box (In & Out)

4. Zoom (multiple options)

5. Fly (yes!)

Of course, APPEAR, RANDOM BARS and DISSOLVE are also good because of their simplicity, but the above animations are recommended when the graphic is enhanced by motion. As we first mentioned, FLY works for objects that actually do move, and you would use it if motion along a path aided your point.

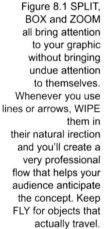

Figure 8.1 SPLIT, BOX and ZOOM all bring attention to your graphic without bringing undue attention to themselves. Whenever you use lines or arrows, WIPE them in their natural irection and you'll create a very professional flow that helps your audience anticipate the concept. Keep FLY for objects that actually travel.

Order & Timing

Once you have determined which animation effect best suits the needs of your visual, you'll want to preview it in the Custom Animation dialogue box. If you have more than one item set to build, you'll also have to set Order and Timing properties to the build to ensure it all happens exactly as you want it to. One sure sign of a hurriedly prepared presentation is when items appear in a chronologically impaired fashion, often to the total consternation of the presenter.

The Order & Timing function gives you total control not only over what happens when, but also a) if the next action will require a mouse click or happen automatically, and b) if so, exactly how long after the last action. With practice, you can design a slide that has multiple builds but requires only one mouse click to set the whole process in motion.

This can make for a very professional-looking show, but only if you make sure you can handle all situations that might occur once you light the wick. For instance, you'll need to know to the second how long you will speak to the last point before the next one appears. You'll also get tripped up if you're hit with a question or other interruption in the middle. We don't suggest you try this with most of your slides, but if you can pull off one or two completely automatic slides without tripping, you'll make a mark on your audience.

Levels and Groupings

But wait, there's more! You're still not done! When animating text, you also need to decide two things: 1) Will you introduce the text All at Once, By Word, or By Letter, and 2) will you group different level Paragraphs together or have each level appear on its own?

Introducing text by word or letter is another brilliant device that the psychopaths in the PowerPoint dungeon conceived to inflict maximum torture on business audiences, and is a leading cause of Death by PowerPoint.

(Try this for fun: Have every word in your slide FLY in from a different direction o n e l e t t e r a t a t i m e !)

If you've designed your slide properly, All at Once works just fine.

Deciding to separate out different paragraph levels is an ad hoc decision, and there is no rule other than the commandment that all actions must work to enhance, rather than detract from, audience comprehension.

Sometimes, to maximize effect, you may want some 2nd or 3rd level paragraphs to appear independently, while others on the same slide appear with their parent levels. In this case, you need to have two separate text boxes, because the properties of Introduce Text hold for the entire text box. With proper alignment and spacing of the words in the separate boxes, the audience need not know they are separate elements.

After Effects

Finally (you're almost done), you have the opportunity to decide what happens after your animation occurs. For the most part, you don't want a sound effect to play, unless it's unique to your concept, and it happens once or twice in your whole presentation. Few things turn-off an audience more than an obnoxious sound repeated ad nauseum.

The After Animation box is where you can do a couple

of useful things. After your item has appeared, you can choose to change its color (if text) or make it disappear altogether, either directly after the animation, or on the next mouse click. Changing the color of the last-appearing line of text can add emphasis to the current line. Having an object disappear may help illustrate more clearly a series of events. Again, these are design choices you need to make depending on what works best for you – you'll only break rules of good design if you overuse.

Curiously, the default for After Animation is "Don't Dim". If you want nothing to happen after each element animates, simply ignore this classic *MicroSpeak*.

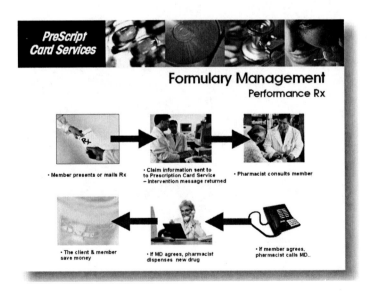

Figure 8.2 The trouble with most "process" slides is that they use static arrows to direct the eye to the next step. The problem is that's exactly what happens – the audience gets caught in an endless loop without stopping to digest any one step.

Telling Your Story

The real advantage to the proper use of animations, or "builds", is that you have enormous control over the way a good story plays out.

Here, we show how we redesigned a client's slide, initially made up of bullet points listing the steps in the prescription control process. Bullet points were able to name the steps, but did little to help the audience imagine the actual actions involved.

Figure 8.3 Instead of arrows, let the scenes themselves direct the audience's eye by appearing only when you're ready to discuss it.

By using pictures that build and then fade as the new step is discussed, we were able to tell a story.

Figure 8.4 The process is now clear and understandable, as people in the audience put themselves in the plot.

Even otherwise dry and technical data, such as that used by presenters in financial, scientific, or technical fields, can come alive and engage an audience when you find a way to form it into a story. Animations help you make the most of the story-building process.

Transitions

In addition to controlling the flow of information within slides using animation, you have similar effects available to you to control the flow from slide to slide. The same rules and observations apply. In other words, many of the transitions work against a smooth and comprehensible presentation, as they draw so much attention to themselves.

There are even software companies out there that will sell you plug-ins to PowerPoint that provide "TV studio" transition effects. Unfortunately, presentations are no more like a TV show than they are like printed documents. The purpose of presentations is information transfer and uptake through a human interface; television is about recreating the human experience through an electronic interface. Reading is about ingesting information at one's own pace; presentations, to be effective, must establish a common pace for many.

A good transition effect is one that prepares the audience for the next slide without causing too much brain damage. Brain damage occurs when the processing power required to deal with the light and motion from the transition is greater than that required to process the information on the new slide. So just as with animations, gentle is better.

Summary

- Builds are the key to total control
- With builds, gentlest is best
- Use builds to Reveal, not to Revel
- Words are more sensitive to movement than graphics
- Transitions: From slide to slide, same rules apply

Chapter 9

Creating Effective Graphs

Making your cases with comparative data

On a Clear Day

Graphs were created to give shape and pattern to numbers, thereby engaging the right brain in the process and speeding comprehension of the data. The left brain filters and interprets information displayed as numbers, rather than ingesting it instantly as when it is graphed.

Yet before we think that this phenomenon means your presentations should include a lot of graphs, we must also realize the limitations the resolution of a computer screen (or LCD projector) place upon displaying graphed information. The goal, of course, is how to graph data in a way that enhances true comprehension.

Edward Tufte doesn't reserve many kind words for Microsoft graphing technology. That's because he sees the information world, or rather the media used to represent information, as a high-resolution, low-resolution continuum. In other words, some media, such as print, with its ability to lay ink on a page at resolutions of 1200 dots per inch, are well suited to bringing clarity to data in the form of a well-designed graph.

But computer screens, with the equivalent "resolution" of perhaps 96 dpi, are not well suited to similar detail. (In Tufte's view, computers have actually "dumbed us down" by their inability to display information anywhere near as clearly as other visual technologies dating back hundreds of years.)

According to many, you commit a grave sin against the gods of design by even *thinking* of using a Microsoft generated graph. So what's a presentation designer to do when faced with the need to display a great deal of numerical data in a way that won't put the audience to sleep?

Legends in their own minds

The first way that Microsoft gets in the way of knowledge transfer, graph-wise, is that it pays more attention to the structure of its charts than to the data the charts are meant to express. That's because at Microsoft, it's always about the *application* (their thing), rather than the *document* (your thing).

When we use the default graphing tool, Microsoft presents us with a 3D bar chart that looks like this:

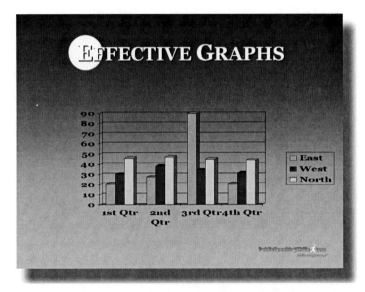

Figure 9.1 The default graph from the resident Graph feature in PowerPoint. Note how the bizarre font and paragraph properties used in the y-axis data labels work so hard to hinder immediate understanding.

What we get is a chart that a) is overloaded with infrastructure such as lines and data labels, and b) a legend that requires a constant back-and-forth view scan in order to know what each element represents.

Note that Microsoft pays zero attention to making the data labels clearly supportive of the data; instead, in their attempt to draw overwhelming attention to themselves, the labels step on each other's toes and obfuscate the fact that we're looking at a simple 1-year timeline.

The lines on the "walls" of the graph aren't really helpful, either, because the "3D" feature makes judging the amount difficult. And then there's the legend. It must be a very important job, being a legend, because how else could you justify taking up almost a quarter of the width of the whole graph?

Legends that are in a separate framework from the graph itself are rarely self-evident. And while they might contain enough information to make them technically self-explanatory, there are certainly better ways to achieve comprehension.

When we dump the infrastructure, we are left with a much clearer view of what the graph is there for – the data!

Figure 9.2 By eliminating the legend, more real estate is available for data. When it comes to data labels, think "Less is More".

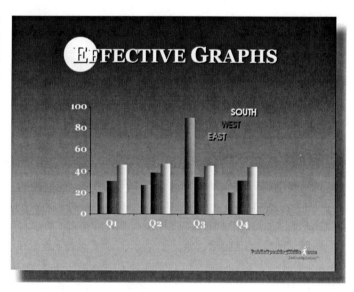

Bits of Knowledge

We don't reject Microsoft quite so out-of-handedly, but you must be aware that the less-is-more principal definitely applies to the subject of graphs and what belongs in them. Furthermore, the amount of information you show is *entirely* media-dependent. Again, from Tufte, here's what you need to know about resolution:

The amount of information that:

the human eye can take in at one time:	150MB
is contained in a large foldout map:	150MB
can be projected on a Kodachrome slide:	35MB
can be displayed on computer CRT:	8MB

This tells us that no matter how much information you need to distribute to your audience, you are going to be very limited by how much you can actually show in your on-screen presentation.

"But the client *demands* that information from our presentation", you say, and you are probably correct. And they're entitled to it. That simply reinforces the argument for the dual-media presentation. Some information simply can't be handled properly by the screen, and therefore must be printed and given in the form a handout. Information that requires scrutiny and the comparison of many details requires that the audience have an opportunity to scan this data at their own pace and with the ability to go over it more than once. That can only be accomplished if the material is in print.

A good printed graph should contain a lot of unambiguous data, and should make it quite clear just what the numbers are and how they relate to one another. You can't do that, for the most part, with an on-screen graph, and still be able to keep the audience all on the same page with you. You certainly can't break the rule that if it's on the screen, you must address it or risk losing the attention of an audience that will attempt to read everything on the screen whether you tell them to or tell them not to.

Have you ever been to a presentation where the presenter puts up completely incomprehensible graph and then says something like "I know you can't read any of this, but I wanted to show you the trend here..."? If your audience can't read it then why purposely give them a headache by putting something on the screen that their curious minds will desperately to *try* to read anyway?

One Step at a Time

So faced with the knowledge that graphs are a good thing in terms of engendering right-brain uptake, yet by their nature contain more information than can be represented properly in the low-resolution computer display environment, what's a designer to do?

You actually have two, non-exclusionary options here that you can use together or by themselves depending upon the complexity of your data.

First, you have the ability to reduce the amount of time your audience spends wandering around the graph looking for true meaning by introducing the elements on at a time, including the axes. This allows you to explain not just the results, but also how you got there. If you are trying to show a classic case of volume over time, you can clearly detail your units of volume as the y-axis appears, and then discuss the history of your time-line (x-axis), all before you introduce the actual data.

Then, you have the option of bringing in the data that your graph displays in a number of ways. In this way, you virtually eliminate all question marks before they arise.

Graph Animation Tip A graph can be animated:

- All at once
- By series (same information)
- By category (by bottom axis)
- By elements in a series
- By elements in a category

To explore all the ways that you can animate graphs in PowerPoint, right click on the graph, select CUSTOM ANIMATION, and then click on the CHART EFFECTS tab. A little experimentation here will go a long way to making your point.

When Clients Insist

Let's remember that the purpose of a presentation is to create enough interest in and respect for your message that your audience will want to know more. In fact, that's really the Holy Grail – to get people to say, even if only to themselves, "Really? Tell me more." Unfortunately, most presentation audiences are saying to themselves, "Oh God, you mean there's *more?*"

With the low resolutions of computer displays, we must approach graphs from the standpoint of trying to tell a story by the shape and relative volume of the elements in each series, rather than trying to get audiences to decipher large groups of numbers attached to the elements.

Showing the actual numbers that your bars or columns or pie wedges represent is worthwhile, but usually only after the audience has had the opportunity to see the general point that the graph is trying to make. In the chart below, you would certainly create a few question marks if we detailed twelve different numbers in the space of the graph itself.

Further, in many cases you do not always know whether your audience really wants all the data, much less for it to be part of the on-screen portion of your presentation.

On the other hand, after you've shown the graph and the audience knows what you're trying to show, it would be nice to be able to get to the details if someone so requested it.

The solution is to have slides with the details hidden in your presentation, and accessed by hyperlinks. For instance, each series could be detailed as such:

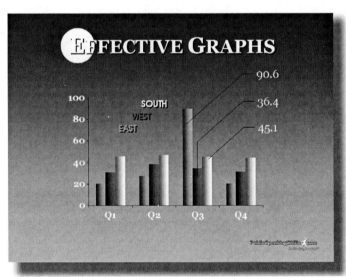

Figure 9.3 When the vice-president calls you out for trying to over-simplify the situation, it's always helpful to have a back-up "reference" slide at the back of your deck to hyperlink to.

To make your navigation easy, you can create an "invisible" box (No Line, No Fill) around the series or category you wish to explore, and use Action Settings to make this box a hyperlinked object to your slide with the additional info. Then set up a return path to the originating slide so you're always returning to the same slide.

Having these details available at the click of your mouse, *but only if you need them,* is an easy way to impress your audience with your thoroughness and professionalism without risking putting them to sleep with minutia they might not have wanted.

The Right Graph

Microsoft does not know a heckuva lot about presentation design, but they do make available different types of graphs so that you can match the graph type to the point you're trying to make with your data. There are twelve different graph types available with PowerPoint 2000, but few of those styles work well in the low-resolution world of computer-based presentations. With few exceptions, here is how you want to use the following types:

- Pie Graphs for Share
- Bar Graphs for Comparative Amounts
- Line Graphs for Trends, Time

Pie Graphs

Pie graphs (commonly misnomered pie *charts*) are one of the more overused, and hence misused, types of graphs, primarily because they are so easy to make, and easy to make look good. They are misused when chosen to show amounts rather than share. The beauty of pie graphs is that they show so clearly what they are supposed to show, i.e., how much of the whole each element contributes. In most cases the actual amounts – in this case percentages – are actually secondary to the area of the slices in terms of telling the story.

When you look at a pie graph with five or fewer slices, your brain can quickly ascertain which groups dominate. We often see pie graphs with more than 5 elements, but they then become more difficult to comprehend in short order. In most cases, consider whether your story needs to include details about all the players, or whether a group of insignificant contributors can be grouped as "others".

If you want to show how much *volume* each element contributes, rather than what *fraction*, you'll want to use a bar graph.

Bar Graphs

To show relative sizes of different segments as well as the actual amounts, you'll want to use a bar graph. Bar graphs are designed to show volumes against a y-axis that clearly delineates the units of measure. By having a series of bars next to each other, we can see how each element compares with the others as well as what absolute volume the element represents.

There are variations on the bar graph, such as a stacked bar, where different elements are stacked on top of each other to form a series, or a 100% bar graph, where all the bars are the same height but are split to show what percent of the whole the volume reflects. In a presentation environment, esoteric options are best to be avoided.

Line Graphs

Line graphs have the unique advantage of speaking to inherent right-brain prejudices about information. That is, when typically conditioned western minds see a graph with no labeling, they automatically assign "volume" to the y-axis, with "up" meaning "more", and a time-line to the x-axis, with the left side meaning most recent. Just as we read from left-to-right, rightward motion subconsciously means positive motion.

You would want to use a line graph, then, to show a progression in amount from one point in time to another. The elevation of the line at any one point represents the quantity of the tracked data at that moment. Audiences, wanting to be the first-to-know, will automatically make assumptions about the types of values x-axes and y-axes represent. Don't disappoint them.

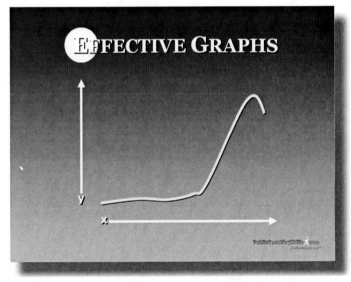

Figure 9.4 Audiences are pre-wired to see "amount" data on the vertical (x) axis, and "time" data on the horizontal. Don't disappoint them.

In the simple, unlabeled graph above, you are likely to assume you are looking at a trend, even though you know nothing about any of the variables. You can imagine, though, some measurement that grew slightly but steadily over a long period of time, then exploded, and is now, thankfully, trending back down. If you guessed that this was the U.S. national deficit from 1950 to 2000, you would be correct.

Graphs are a great way of making complex information easily understood. But graphs work best only when you fully integrate words, numbers and images. Whenever possible, label the elements of your graph directly on the elements, if you can do so without cluttering the "picture" a good graph can make. If you can't, make separate images of the same chart and hyperlink to them to show specific data clearly.

Don't make your audience have to learn your system. If you require a complicated legend, you and your audience will both be lost.

Figure 9.5 Of course, you always have to first ask yourself if the data is worth the time and trouble of making a graph.

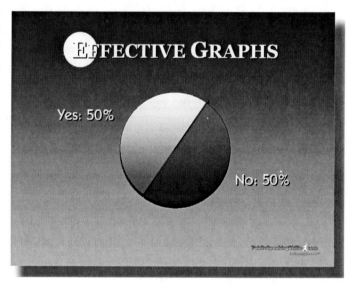

Finally, make sure your information is worth graphing in the first place. Even a well-designed graph cannot be a substitute for lack of good data.

"A man's got to know his limitations."
- Dirty Harry

Summary

- For clarity, integrate legends and think right-brain
- Subdue Infrastructure – let your data shine
- Pie Graphs for Share
- Bar Graphs for Comparative Amounts
- Line Graphs for Trends, Time

Chapter 10

On Edward Tufte

and Conquering Death
by Powerponit

Very early on the morning of January, 2003, seven astronauts aboard the Space Shuttle Columbia were circling the earth, donning their gear, and looking forward to coming home after 12 days in space. They were not aware, nor would they ever be aware, that back on earth a debate had been raging at various levels inside and outside of NASA over the advisability of clearing Columbia for re-entry. Boeing engineers in the ad hoc Debris Assessment Team had been fruitlessly seeking the ear of persons of authority in the Mission Management Team, in a desperate attempt to get them to understand that a catastrophe might quickly unfold.

These highly educated people, these engineers, or rather, theses *rocket scientists*, had tried to convince their superiors, technically *executive rocket scientists*, that a 1.67-pound block of high-tech Styrofoam had likely inflicted enough damage to either the protective tiles or the wing to put into question the ship's survivability upon contact with the super-heated gases that would soon be created by friction with the atmosphere.

Sadly, the seven souls aloft had put their faith in rocket science, when what they really needed was a neurosurgeon. The neurosurgeon would have at least understood that the human brain, being neatly sliced in two as it is, is often much more susceptible to persuasion when presented with right-brain type information rather than the strictly (and even over-the-top) left-brain evidence that the rocket scientists had used to no avail.

Over the course of five days, the Debris Assessment Team had delivered three presentations, consisting of a total of 28 slides that attempted to show that they had studied both the evidence available about Columbia and the evidence on all the foam that had ever fallen off any of the previous shuttles. This spray-on foam insulation, referred to in the slides as SOFI, had been known to flake off from the main fuel tank under the rigors of takeoff for almost a decade. The errant foam was almost always from the areas where complicated surfaces required its application be done manually, rather than by the precise computer-controlled process that applied the foam to the other 99.9 percent of the tank.

One of these areas, known as the "bipod ramp" and referred to in the presentations as simply the "ramp", was unfortunately well-suited to commit major damage with flying foam owing to its location near the forward tip of the shuttle. Foam detaching from this point, given the relative speed of the shuttle in its path, could strike with a force exceeding that of a brick shot from a cannon at short range. Unfortunately, the physics involved here were unknown to even Shuttle program manager Ronald Dittemore. Dittemore was the face and voice of NASA to the world in the first week after the accident, until he revealed a lack of respect for scientific inquiry during a press conference by holding up a sample of SOFI and saying, in effect, to said world, "I'm sorry, but nobody's ever going to convince me that a piece of foam could bring down a space shuttle!"

And although the problem of foam debris at takeoff had been significant enough to have NASA commission a test, referred to in the slide as Crater, the rocket scientists suspected that the current parameters of the problem were not like what they had studied before.

The mindset in place with the NASA Mission Management Team at the time was that yes, we know foam falls off and damages tiles, but that is an issue of maintenance, not safety-of-flight. Let's not worry our pretty little heads about the extra work the clean-up crews will have with the ship when she returns to the hanger.

It is apparent from the volume of information in the slides that the Boeing rocket scientists had done an admirable job of researching the problem. And having conducted such exhaustive research, it is reasonable to assume that they thought they were doing their job by presenting ALL of it to the people who would ultimately decide if their take on the evidence was sound.

First, a little perspective

Before we go on, however, it's essential to first note two things.

First, the slide you're about to see was originally brought to popular attention by none other than the distinguished Dr. Tufte mentioned so often throughout this text. Dr. Tufte was actually asked by the Columbia Accident Investigation Board to scour documents relevant to the investigation and render his opinion on whether the design of such documents may have played a role in what turned out to be some errant decision-making. Dr. Tufte had some years earlier demonstrated that a Pre-PowerPoint era (was there ever such a time?) presentation had, through its lack of a coherent design, helped to doom *Challenger*.

Dr. Tufte has taken up a crusade, or perhaps *jihad*, to rally against the use of PowerPoint for serious and technical presentations, correctly pointing out the limitations of its ability to aid true knowledge transfer when used, as it was, in this now infamous "Boeing" slide. We often joke that Dr. Tufte believes that someday, the wrong person will give the wrong PowerPoint presentation to the wrong audience, and the world will come to an end!

Our issue with Tufte's assessment of the evil of PowerPoint is the old one that guns don't kill people, presenters do. PowerPoint, like a gun, or a car or a surgical instrument is dangerous in untrained hands – hardly a call for worldwide eradication. Tufte is a brilliant, charismatic performer on the platform, and can actually present well even when having his audience read along with him from one of his beautifully crafted textbooks.

For the far less-talented rest of us, PowerPoint can be a fantastic tool that adds visual interest and understanding while serving as an excellent content-management system.

The second point we need to make relates to the first, and that is this: we hold no one involved in the creation of these "Boeing" slides accountable for the tragic result of the lack of communication that permeated the management levels of NASA in 2003. We are relatively certain that none of the rocket scientists there had ever taken a professionally-developed training course in proper presentation design. Look around today and you'll be hard-pressed to find much more than a class or two by some firm that will take your ugly, unpresentable slides and make them over into pretty, unpresentable slides.

The answer to the PowerPoint problem is simple: education. Business people and rocket scientists alike simply need to be trained in the elements of presentation design before putting their PowerPoint files on automatic and senselessly firing away at their audiences. PowerPoint is too deeply inculturated into our professional lives to be either banned (Tufte) or considered workable without training (most businesses).

It's actually a shame that Microsoft hasn't stepped up to the plate and at least used its considerable array of bully pulpits to defend the good intent of it product while acknowledging the need for universal training for its users. And we're of course not talking about PowerPoint 101, but rather Design 101, courses that would give users the required background in what works and what doesn't when projecting information to humans on the big screen. Perhaps the Mountain View gang's self-imposed exile has kept them once removed from the watchful eye of Redmond, and this glaring lack of understanding of their own product's needs is an oversight that might come back to bite them someday.

In any case, let's take a look at this very real, very tragic slide, and then offer up an alternative to the presentation's design, rather than once again blame the software for the limitations of its users.

Before we address the issues with this slide, we'd like you to have a fighting chance to see for yourself whether or not the slide works to achieve true knowledge transfer. Knowledge transfer typically requires that the presenter and every member of the audience remain on the same page, on the same wavelength, really, every step of the way. For that to occur, the presenter needs to know some basics about the delivery process, the content of the presentation must hold some pertinent interest for the audience members, and the slide must abide by some basic rules.

So one last time, let's review:

1. Favor Right-Brain information
2. K.I.S.S. - Less is More
3. One concept per visual
4. Use proper builds
5. Be colorful - Light on dark
6. Avoid boring fonts
7. Maintain paragraph integrity

Keep these rules in mind as you attempt to find the data whose importance was clearly lost in the translation.

Ready?

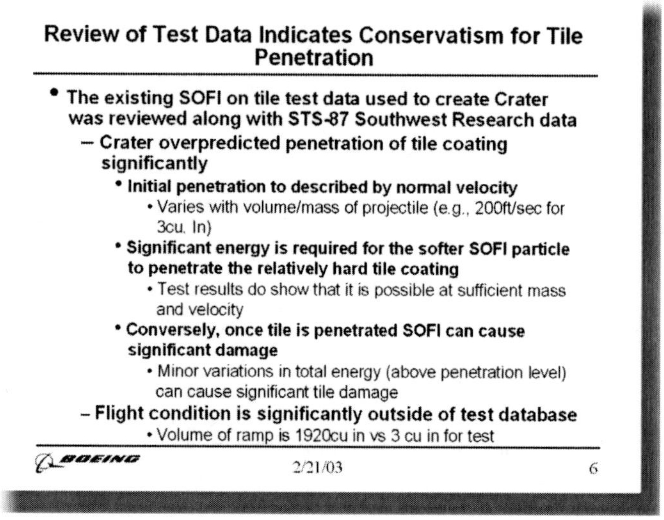

Figure 10.1 Slide 6 of a 12 slide presentation to the Mission Management Team and others. Yes, the other 11 looked just like it.

Review of Test Data Indicates Conservatism for Tile Penetration

- The existing SOFI on tile test data used to create Crater was reviewed along with STS-87 Southwest Research data
  - Crater overpredicted penetration of tile coating significantly
    - Initial penetration to described by normal velocity
      - Varies with volume/mass of projectile (e.g., 200ft/sec for 3cu. In)
    - Significant energy is required for the softer SOFI particle to penetrate the relatively hard tile coating
      - Test results do show that it is possible at sufficient mass and velocity
    - Conversely, once tile is penetrated SOFI can cause significant damage
      - Minor variations in total energy (above penetration level) can cause significant tile damage
  - Flight condition is significantly outside of test database
    - Volume of ramp is 1920cu in vs 3 cu in for test

BOEING   2/21/03   6

When we present this slide in our presentation design classes, we set a stopwatch when it first appears and then note at what times eyeballs depart from the fray and start looking elsewhere for comfort. People start giving up at about 45-seconds; those determined to slug it out usually take a minute and 15. Isn't there a rule about 10 seconds? Doesn't *Less is More* hold within it a rule that your visual shouldn't include more information than it takes the normal person 10 seconds or less to comprehend?

But wait, we're getting ahead of ourselves again. Let's start at the bottom and work our way up.

Maintain paragraph integrity

Well, it's hard to mess with paragraph integrity when you're only working with one slide, but this one violates the tenets of the rule by disrespecting the fact that the viewer is going to assume the most important information will be delivered in the largest type. Here, as you'll soon see, the only bit of truly actionable data is presented in the smallest font size.

Avoid boring fonts

Could you be more guilty of really bad design than to use Arial in black against a white background? All 28 slides in the 3 presentations designed by the rocket scientists used this comprehension-killing approach. Is it a wonder why none of the serious data stuck with the people trying to view 28 slides that look like this? They more or less massacre the 6 X 6 rule here, too, stroking 17 body text lines with an average of 8 (and as many as 12) words per line.

Be Colorful

Covered, don't you think?

Use proper builds

Well, you can't *mis*use builds if you don't build at all, but in this case they clearly break the rule by bringing on 17 lines of text all at once, without a chance for anyone to decipher one bit of information before being hit with the next. In this case, parceling alone might have saved the day by bringing forth that one bit of important data with its own time and attention slot.

One concept per visual

We stopped counting the number of concepts when it got to 6, but the damage here is even more severe. Note that at the first dash-shaped "bullet", we're told that "Crater over predicted penetration of tile coating significantly." But three dots later, we learn that "Conversely, once tile is penetrated SOFI can cause significant damage." So not only do we have more than *one* concept, we have *conflicting* concepts presented at the same time. You know you're in trouble when you see the word "Conversely" in the middle of the slide. Again, the only concept that means anything at all here lies buried beneath an avalanche of other concepts.

Less is More

If the rocket scientists had used more judicious tabbing and reduced the indents of the bullets by a half-inch or more, it is possible they could have filled the *entire* slide with words. Always next time.

And finally,

Favor right-brain information

Here is where any hope of knowledge transfer dies in the quagmire of the slide. Of all the ways they might have presented the one set of data that means anything, the one piece of actionable information that should have bowled the executive rocket scientists over mercilessly, their one shot at slam-dunking their argument, they chose instead to

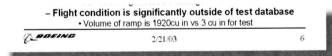

Figure 10.2 All the worthwhile, actionable data in the entire slide lies in one line at the bottom, rendered in, of course, the smallest font size used.

ask themselves, "How can we make this information more *left*-brained". Rocket scientists, people whose job it is to be a little more technical than "righty-tighty, lefty-loosey", got this whole right-brain, left-brain thing mixed up and converted what might have been as simple as a 1-column, 2 number chart into a full blown left-brain sentence, and killed all chance for comprehension as surely as hot cosmic gases blowtorching through Columbia killed the good men and women inside.

If you haven't figured it out yet, the story in the slide is all in the very last line. In fact, the entire slide – no, make that the entire presentation – could have been, should have been thrown in the hopper and reduced to one simple graphic. One simple graphic can say all that needed to be said about the situation to know that a catastrophe was, indeed, 100% predictable.

And tragically still, none of the points that the rocket scientists were trying to make needed to be misunderstood. In other words, without changing any of the data or eliminating any of the information, though that certainly wouldn't hurt, the same presentation could have been given, and the audience could have agreed with their argument, if only the slides had stuck to the rules.

Columbia data by the rules

Although much has been written about how this one slide demonstrates the need to banish PowerPoint from all serious meetings, we take a different, and, we think, much more practical tack. With installations in the literally hundreds of millions, PowerPoint is not about to disappear overnight, nor are people who are tasked to report to higher-ups on what they've been up to lately likely to begin crafting lengthy word documents with footnotes and citations.

We believe, in fact, that had the rocket scientists been educated in proper presentation design, they could have made such a compelling case for caution that no one in that fateful meeting room would have thought twice about going ahead with re-entry. Used properly, the simple graphics capability of this simple program can convey concepts of the most complicated origin.

The first job of fixing this mess was to apply a few basic right-brain friendly touches such as color, an image, and a less than boring (in fact, appropriate-to-the-setting) font. Then we tore the slide apart so that all the data on each slide was relevant to all the other data on the slide, and when we ran out of data, we went to – are you ready? – a NEW slide. Just as time goes by just fine even when not filled by your talking (a key concept behind The Pause), slide backgrounds need not be filled with words for them to function.

Please note that for the sake of reader interest, we've offered a synopsis of each slide to suggest its true underlying meaning. But by doing so, we're definitely NOT suggesting that the person *delivering* this presentation offer up anything less than what appears on the screen. Remember, if you feel it's important enough to include in the slide, you MUST address it, and leave no bullet points "orphaned". You can always say more than what's up there, but never less.

Figure 10.3 Synopsis: When we first looked at the data on possible damage to the orbiter from flying foam, it appeared as if it were unlikely.

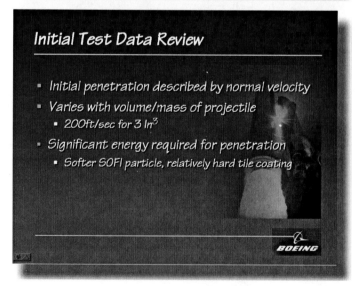

Initial Test Data Review

- Tile Penetration Unlikely
  - CRATER test data on SOFI reviewed
  - Southwest Research STS-87 data examined
  - Tests significantly over-predicted penetration

BOEING

Figure 10.4 Synopsis: Actual damage is a function of basic physics; tests used a foam particle about the size of a golf ball traveling at 300 mph. Intuition suggests a throwaway coffee cup couldn't damage baked enamel.

Initial Test Data Review

- Initial penetration described by normal velocity
- Varies with volume/mass of projectile
  - 200ft/sec for 3 In^3
- Significant energy required for penetration
  - Softer SOFI particle, relatively hard tile coating

BOEING

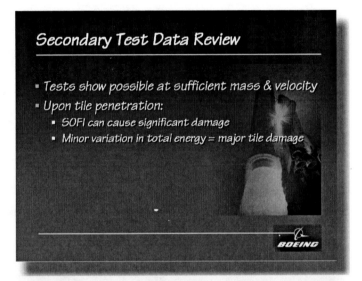

Figure 10.5
Synopsis: Further, deeper review of the data showed that if you have a big enough piece of foam traveling at a good enough clip, you actually can mess up somebody's day.

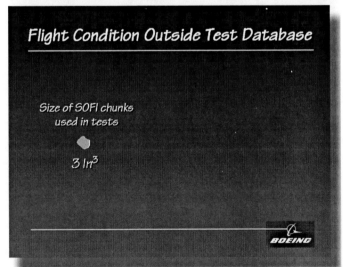

Figure 10.6
Synopsis: You know all that stuff we just showed you to impress you with the breadth and depth of our knowledge? Forget it – for the situation at hand, it don't mean squat.

And with a flick of the headline:

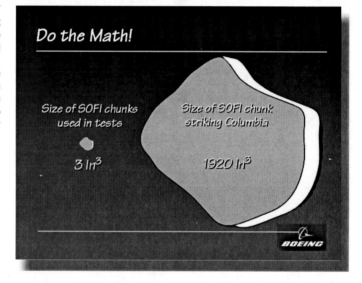

When we show this set of slides in class, and ask our students if anyone would have elected to bring the Columbia down after seeing the argument put this way, it's usually a fait accompli – no one sides with NASA. We then ask if anyone in the room is a rocket scientist, and very few raise their hands. (Of course, when our audience was a group of brain surgeons, we had a number of alternative responses.)

The point is, of course, that one not need be a rocket scientist to be persuaded by right-brain information.

Edward Tufte would have the rocket scientists share their information with others through the use of heavily foot-noted written documents, which is an admirable approach. Not very realistic today, but nevertheless admirable.

And yet it is strikingly clear in this slide that PowerPoint *can* function quite adequately when attempting to make an argument based on data, if only that data is represented in a way that is unambiguous to even the casual observer. Casual observers tend to skip the footnotes.

The role of the presentation designer (and this is a role that in most cases should be assumed, at least in part, by the presenter herself) is not to ensure that the presentation includes all the relevant data. The responsibility of the designer must be to ensure that the audience *receives* the data, and receives it in such an unambiguous way that all eyes are seeing exactly what the presenter has in mind. Ironically, PowerPoint is a tool uniquely suited to do just that. We believe this last slide would have sent such a message, and more strongly and more unambiguously to the assembled audience than any scholarly dissertation Dr. Tufte would have been able to assemble.

In truth, a properly designed on-screen presentation should never attempt to take the place of well-researched and well-written, grammatically full and correct printed documents. As we've mentioned before, a problem with the common PowerPoint culture in most businesses today is the misconception that the same document can serve both functions – the projected program and the takeaway. Those two functions could not be more diametrically opposed, and yet we still see "edicts" from on high proscribing design rules that are meant to work for the printed form – all at the expense of deliverability from the screen.

Virtually all of the problems we see with corporate presentations can be traced to the misguided belief that somehow a software program invented to lesson a presenter's dependence on the graphics department can now *by decree* be the universal document production software for all information transfer – and that all knowledge transfer shall be conducted through ONE document, regardless of whether its for group or individual consumption.

Could you imagine if Steven Spielberg set out to make a movie of a Steven King book, and then used the book itself as the screenplay? Would you sit through a 12-hour movie, with voice-over narration taking the place of visual images?

Books and movies can tell the same story, but each according the rules and structures that work for each artform. Why should presentations be considered any differently?

So it is true of words as it is with sunbeams.
The more concentrated,
the deeper the burn.
- Unknown

Summary

- PowerPoint doesn't kill people; bad design does
- No matter your audience, right brains rule
- The designer's role is to ensure the message is *received*
- As always, proper education is key

Chapter 11

Going Forward

If you've made it this far, you no doubt have ascertained that we take the rules of proper presentation design pretty seriously. And we do! We have developed our strong feelings about design because we've been privileged to train thousands of business people in the art of presentation delivery, and have thus had a unique perspective on the inextricable relationship between delivery and design.

Every year, we meet and train people who have come to us because of the difficulty they've had in either feeling comfortable or persuasive while standing up before a group. Few things are more rewarding for us than to see their epiphany when they finally understand that so many of their problems centered around trying to translate what they had on the screen to the bewildered gaze of their audience. As is true about many tasks we're required to perform in the course of business, when we don't do things well we think it's our fault.

Just edit!

Everybody who comes to our training room admits to be nervous when presenting, and most think that their anxiety reflects a weakness in *them*. So when they leave our training armed with the ability to finally perform this special skill well, we both feel great. In every case, though, they realize that none of the skills that we train such as eye contact, gestures, inflection, timing and so forth will really be of help without the ability to design slides that work.

At the risk of making a sweeping generalization that might not pertain to your last presentation, your slides could probably lose 50% of your verbiage, and your talk could lose 50% of its content, without losing any of its impact. In other words, edit, edit, edit. Like this book, which took much longer to edit than it did to write, documents usually get better with every pass, especially if you have the discipline to cut anything that looks or sounds the slightest bit unnecessary.

Give me your answer in the morning...

If you can "sleep" on your presentation, or anything you write, so much the better – bullets and charts that you deemed absolutely essential two days ago often lose their importance once you've stepped away from them for a while.

And while you're trimming away those branches, ask yourself if your audience might not be able to see more of your real story if you chopped down a tree or two in the way. Remember: How well you look and sound when you deliver, the parts that carry almost all the impact of the presentation, depends mostly on how deeply you understand and how strongly you feel about the subject.

You can't be expressive, you can't be passionate, about 12 different streams of information. You can be about 3.

Wherever you go, there you are!

Finally, always remember that the presentation does not take place on the screen, nor does it form at the presenter's mouth. Presentations only ever occur in one place, and that's in the mind of the individual audience member. Depending on what their left-brain filters allow to pass through, each member therefore experiences a slightly different presentation. Your job is to make sure that what they really need to see and hear not just gets through, but gets remembered as well. People can't remember a lot of new things that they hear for the first time. They can remember a few things that they hear several times, especially if they feel some emotion behind the arguments.

Keep it simple, keep it short, show how much you care. Hey – maybe that's all we ever needed to say!

Summary

- Keep it simple
- Keep it short
- Show how much you care
- Avoid redundancy

Index

Bibliography

Arnheim, Rudolf. *Art and Visual Perception.* U of C Press, 1974.

Buckley, Reid. *Strictly Speaking.* McGraw Hill, 1999.

Cabbage, Michael & Harwood, Michael. *Comm Check...* Free Press, 2004

Dondis, Donis A. *A Primer of Visual Literacy.* MIT Press, 1973

Gardner, Howard. *Multiple Intelligences.* Perseus, 1993

Gardner, Howard. *Art, Mind & Brain.* Perseus, 1982

Hoff, Ron. *I Can See You Naked.* Andrews & McMeel, 1988

Kahrs, Till. *Enhancing Your Presentation Skills.* IUniverse. 1999.

Noonan, Peggy. *Simply Speaking.* Regan Books, 1998.

Norman, Donald. *The Design of Everyday Things.* Doubleday/Currency, 1988.

Ornstein, Robert. *The Right Mind.* Harcourt Brace,

1997.

Stumpf, Bill. *The Ice Palace That Melted Away*. Pantheon Books, 1998.

Tufte, Edward. *Envisioning Information.*. The Graphics Press, 2001.

Tufte, Edward. *The Visual Display of Quantitative Information*. The

Graphics Press, 2001.

Tufte, Edward. *Visual Explanations*. The Graphics Press, 2001.

Underhill, Roy. *Krushchev's Shoe*. Perseus Publishing, 2000.

Williams, Robin. *The Non-Designers Design Book*. PeachPit Press, 1994.

Acknowledgements

As is true with most worthwhile projects, this book required the contributory efforts of a number of good people.

The brilliant TV journalist Jill Chernekoff was gracious enough to edit an early rendition of this book; we cannot hold her responsible for any oversights in the final draft.

I'd like to thank Till Kahrs for his continuous hounding (I think he'd call it persistent persuasion) to finish the darn thing, and to the strategic insights of the ever-professional Claire Baillargeon, for helping me believe that I could. Claire was also most helpful in providing perception to the PowerPoint cultures of many large corporations and organizations.

The more-talented-than-she-knows graphic artist Traci Watson showed me the road to good layout, as well as provide me with understanding of her design theories and how they can help the presentation designer.

Dennis Austin, one of the originators of PowerPoint, was kind enough to share images of his collection of the all the various iterations of the product packaging from the early Mac product to the present.

Finally, this volume would never have gotten to press without my having a place to retreat from the realities of the office for an extended time and be left alone with my thoughts and my keypad. For that I shall be forever grateful to Greg Landis, who, to this day, retains the distinction of being the most eligible bachelor in the equestrian societies of both Philadelphia's Main Line and West Palm Beach. Greg's beautiful winter home on the show grounds in Wellington, Florida provided an idyllic retreat for an undisciplined writer to have no excuses but to put pen to paper day after day, from early morning to late at...well, let's just say cocktail hour.

Thank-you, all.

About the Author

J. Douglas Jefferys' diverse background includes the automotive industry, manufacturing, global marketing & information technology.

A Microsoft Certified Professional, Doug began his platform-training career in 1981 with Commodore Business Machines. There, Doug was challenged to present what was then a hobbyist's concept - the PC - as a viable new consumer product. To best showcase features and functionality, Doug learned BASIC and built from scratch what would be one of the first on-screen presentations.

Fully 10 years *before* Windows 3.0, Doug was helping to create the ground rules for successful computer-based presentation techniques. Today, in addition to training thousands of satisfied participants in proper public speaking skills, Doug continues to develop and edit dynamic on-screen presentations for top executives at many Fortune 500 companies.

One of Doug's greatest skills is his ability to help people build confidence in just being themselves when speaking to a group. With a coaching style that is based on straight talk and proper doses of humor, Doug is known for getting participants to freely give their maximum in a non-intimidating way. Technical types often comment that their sessions were the first time they felt good talking to people's faces instead of to their shoes! (Doug comes from a family of engineers, so he knows…)

At 29, Doug pursued a unique career-path change, joining the U.S. Army and enrolling in helicopter flight school. He is now an avid fixed-wing pilot, and in keynote speeches shares his "late-life" basic training experience and the challenges he leaned to overcome to achieve his goals

Contact: Doug@publicspeakingskills.com

ISBN 141209241-8

9 781412 092418